The American Sign Language Phrase Book

Lou Fant and Barbara Bernstein Fant

Illustrations by Betty G. Miller

Mc
Graw
Hill

New York Chicago San Francisco Lisbon London Madrid Mexico City
Milan New Delhi San Juan Seoul Singapore Sydney Toronto

16 17 18 19 20 LCR 21 20 19 18   (0-07-149713-7)
11 12 13 14 15 16 17 18 19 20 LCR 21 20 19 18   (0-07-175930-1)

ISBN 978-0-07-175932-8 (book and DVD set)
MHID   0-07-175932-8

ISBN 978-0-07-175930-4 (book for set)
MHID   0-07-175930-1

ISBN 978-0-07-149713-8 (book alone)
MHID   0-07-149713-7

e-ISBN 978-0-07-164235-4
e-MHID   0-07-164235-8

Interior design by Monica Baziuk

McGraw-Hill books are available at special quantity discounts to use as premiums and sales promotions or for use in corporate training programs. To contact a representative, please e-mail us at bulksales@mcgraw-hill.com.

This book is printed on acid-free paper.

I dedicate this edition to my beloved sister, Frances Petersen,
who will not survive the ravages of cancer.

—Barbara Bernstein Fant

Contents

Hello. • Good morning. • Good afternoon. • Good night. • How are you? • How have you been? • I'm glad to see you. • See you later. • Good-bye. • I feel fine. • Additional vocabulary • I haven't seen you for a long time. • Thank you. • Please. • No, thank you. • Pardon me. • Where is the restroom? • Close/open the door/window. • Do you like to watch TV? • Do you want to go to the movies? • What's your phone number? • Do you have a TTY? • Do you have a car? • May I go with you? • Have a seat, please. • What time is it? • I have to go home. • Where are you going? • I'm sorry. • Have a nice Thanksgiving. • Merry Christmas. • Happy Hanukkah. • Happy New Year. • Happy birthday.

month. • Call the ambulance. • Do you have hospitalization insurance?
• I have an appointment at 2:30. • Where's my toothbrush? • I want to
brush my teeth. • I already took a bath/shower. • Wash your hands/face. •
I haven't shaved yet. • May I borrow your hair dryer? • Brush your hair. •
I lost my comb.

7 | Weather — 143

It's beautiful today. • The sun is hot. • I enjoy sitting in the sun.
• It was cold this morning. • It will freeze tonight. • Maybe it will snow
tomorrow. • There was thunder and lightning last night. • It rained
yesterday. • Do you have a raincoat? • I lost my umbrella. • Where are
your galoshes/rubbers? • It's windy today. • Yesterday evening at sunset,
the clouds were beautiful. • I hope it clears up this afternoon. • I like
spring/summer/autumn/winter best. • You have to have chains to
drive in the mountains in winter. • I'm afraid of tornados. • What's the
temperature? • Has the snow melted? • There was a flood last year. • The
temperature is below zero. • Have you ever been in an earthquake?

8 | Family — 155

Your father is nice looking. • You look like your mother. • My
brother is younger than I. • My sister speaks several languages fluently. •
His son wants to be an astronaut. • Her daughter works here. • My uncle
is a farmer. • My aunt lives in town. • Your nephew gave me a book. •
His niece will help you. • Her grandfather gave her grandmother a book.
• My cousin is a pilot. • Who is that man? • Did you see the woman? •
The baby is cute. • The girl told the boy that she loves him. • Father told
the little boy to play outside. • The little girl's doll is broken. • How many
children are coming? • Our family is large/small. • We had a family
reunion last summer. • We met at Grandfather's farm. • Additional
vocabulary

9 | School — 173

Do you go to school?/Are you in school? • I go to college. • I'm
majoring in English. • Additional vocabulary for majors or courses of
study • Special education • Physical therapy • Computer science •
What course are you taking this semester? • I'm a student. • Additional

vocabulary. • I graduated last year. • I'm in graduate school now. • I like to study. • Where's the administration building? • You've got to go to the library and do some research. • I got an A on my paper. • I studied all night. • Where's my calculator? • My roommate and I live in a dorm. • I have a question. • Did you ask him? • The teacher asked me a lot of questions. • No talking during the test. • We have a test tomorrow. • Close/open your books. • Begin/stop writing. • I lost my pencil. • Please don't erase the board. • Did you pass or fail/flunk? • Any questions? • You haven't turned in your paper to me yet. • She and I discussed it. • Let's take a break. • When you've been absent, you must bring an excuse.

10 | Food and Drink — 193

Have you eaten?/Did you eat?/Are you finished eating? • I haven't eaten yet. • He eats too much. • Are you hungry? • Let's you and I go to a restaurant. • What are you going to order? • Do you want a cocktail? • Do you want red or white wine? • I'll have a scotch and water. • They have a lot of different beers. • He never drinks whiskey. • Do you want a soft drink? • I want a tall Coke/Pepsi. • I like sandwiches and hamburgers. • Where's the waiter/waitress? • The service is lousy. • I've been waiting 20 minutes. • I want a large/medium/small milk. • I'll have iced/hot tea. • I'll have coffee after I eat. • Do you want milk/cream and sugar? • I take it black, please. • Sugar only/both, please. • The food is delicious. • The meat is too rare. • He/she does not eat meat. He/she's a vegetarian. • The vegetables are overdone. • Additional vocabulary • Breakfast • Lunch • Supper/dinner • Scrambled • Soft-/hard-boiled eggs • Eggs sunny-side up • Eggs over easy

11 | Clothing — 218

I have to go shopping. • What are you wearing tonight? • That dress is an odd color. • Do you have any dirty clothes? • I need to do some laundry. • Is there a laundromat nearby? • He always dresses nicely. • The shirt and tie don't match. • Blue agrees with you. • My trousers are torn. • Can you sew a button for me? • I can't tie a bow tie. • Most women wear slacks nowadays. • Shirt and shoes are required. • I wear shorts every day in the summer. • She needs to wash out her skirt. • Your socks don't

18 | Technology — 330

I have e-mail. • Would you mind giving me your e-mail address? • Which Internet service provider do you use? AOL or MSN? • Do you have cable TV? • Where's the remote? • I do not have cable service. • He/she has a high-definition TV. • Please fax me your résumé. • I bought a laptop. • What make is your computer? • How much memory does your computer have? • I don't have high-speed Internet access. • Copy and paste your document. • Download this program. • Have you printed your document? • My printer is broken. • Please save your file. • I accidentally deleted my file. • Did you scan your photograph? • Send your picture as an attachment. • My computer crashed! • A virus destroyed my hard drive. • Which software do you prefer? • Please burn a CD. • I will buy a DVD/VHS player. • A satellite dish is expensive! • My camcorder works fine. • My parents gave me a 35-mm digital camera for my birthday. • My aunt got a GPS for her boat. • iPods are very popular! • That coffeehouse doesn't have wi-fi access. • What's the link to that blog? • This theater downtown has open captioning. • My TV has closed captioning. • Which pager did you choose? • I need to recharge my pager. • Mine's a BlackBerry pager. • I will buy a Sidekick III pager. • I love video relay service! • A few people use the voice carryover feature on the video relay service. • When you get home, check your video relay mail. • The wireless Internet relay on my pager is terrific! • Sometimes I use the IP relay on my computer. • Deaf people text message their hearing friends. • Some deaf people have gotten cochlear implants. • How do you feel about cochlear implants? • My deaf-blind friend has a closed-circuit television magnifier. • Did you see that vlog? • Most deaf people use light-signaling devices for their doorbells, alarm clocks, videophones, and TTYs, and to alert them to a baby's cry. • Nowadays, deaf people are using video relay services rather than TTYs.

Preface to the Third Edition

In 1983, Lou Fant set out to create an American Sign Language phrase book that made communication easier by presenting common and frequently used phrases. For the hearing world, *The American Sign Language Phrase Book* became an indispensable aid to signing, skipping formal grammatical exercises and vocabulary lists in favor of simply presenting everyday phrases—with a concise section on the grammatical components, sentence structure, and other unique features of ASL. An added bonus was the illustrations, by the nationally renowned deaf artist Betty Miller, which were accessible and detailed without being complicated—and which featured a stylized version of Lou!

A second edition was published in 1994 that incorporated additional vocabulary signs used by deaf people of other nationalities, in particular. More elaboration on these signs can be found in Chapter 13, "Travel." New discoveries were made about ASL grammar, which was expanded upon in the second edition. That edition was a success as much as the first book. Combined sales of both editions reached the 250,000 mark!

I must sadly report that my husband, Lou Fant, died in 2001. An internationally known man of many talents, Lou was indeed a rare breed, and his demise was widely mourned by many. He was truly a great ambassador between the deaf and hearing worlds, leaving the *Phrase Book* as part of his legacy.

Inevitably, though, there was a need in the intervening 14 years since the second edition to bring the *Phrase Book* up to date. Technology is now a big part of everyone's lives, and this third edition acknowledges that role in Chapter 18, an entirely new chapter featuring more than 50 phrases incorporating technologies such as e-mail, video relay services, closed captioning, and more. Once again, we've used the artistic expertise of Betty Miller to render the new phrases (this time with a stylized version of me). Also in this third edition, phrases were vetted to ensure they were still important for common use.

Since technology sign concepts were a fairly recent addition to ASL, I enlisted the aid of some dear friends and colleagues to arrive at a consensus of what signs were used by deaf people throughout the United States. (Please keep in mind there will be some regional sign differences in certain parts of the country.)

For their invaluable input and rather lively and spirited discussions, I extend my heartfelt gratitude to

Randy Bessner, Pagan A. Thomsen, Lisa J. Berke, Kellie McComas, Brenda Aron, John Plecher, Nat Wilson, Christine Visser, Eric Scheir, and Adam Novsam.

Helen and Arthur Novsam, Adam's hearing parents who chanced to be in Seattle for a visit and gladly offered some popular technology phrases.

Brenda Bessner, for the long, countless hours she spent painstakingly taking pictures of every sign concept and transferring more than a thousand of these photos to CDs.

Aline Smith and Laura Harvey for their artistic input on the cover of the third edition.

Dr. Marina McIntire, my former professor at California State University–Northridge and friend, for her perusal of the second edition and suggested changes.

Nancy Creighton, for her invaluable assistance with the new art.

Kristi Winter and Katie Roberts, for their gracious linguistic input on ASL.

Holly McGuire at McGraw-Hill, for her guidance, patience, and
 diplomacy throughout this project.

Bee, Fern, Marie, Lisa, Kristen, and Nancy, my sisters in spirit.

Lou, Dad, and Diana: thank you always for your love, support,
 and guidance in the past. Like you said, let the universe take
 care of itself.

I hope you will find this third edition of *The American Sign Language Phrase Book* to be as worthy and helpful as the previous two
editions. Best wishes and happy learning!

—Barbara Bernstein Fant

How to Use This Book

AMERICAN SIGN LANGUAGE, commonly abbreviated to ASL and occasionally known as Ameslan, is the sign language most deaf people use when they are communicating among themselves. It has its own grammatical structure, which differs from English grammar. You must approach ASL in the same manner you would approach any foreign language—do not expect ASL to be like English or to conform to rules of English grammar. (For a more detailed discussion of the grammatical structure of ASL, see Chapter 2.) Do not ask why ASL, or any language, has a certain structure; ask only how it works. It does no good at all to ask Spanish-speaking people, for example, why they put adjectives after nouns; they just do, and you must accept that. Some of the constructions in ASL may seem odd to you at first because they depart radically from the way we say things in English, but after a while they will seem as natural as English.

It is a common misconception that ASL is merely the fingerspelling of English words. Fingerspelling—using the manual alphabet to spell out entire words letter by letter—is occasionally incorporated into ASL, but the vocabulary of ASL consists of signs. (See the Appendix for a complete treatment of this manual alphabet.)

The format of this book is not that of a traditional foreign language textbook. There are no formal grammatical exercises or drills, and there are no vocabulary lists to memorize. Rather, this book is a guide to conversation with deaf people. It contains phrases, expressions, sentences, and questions that come up in casual, everyday conversations. These phrases enable you to begin talking with deaf people without first having to master the grammar of the language.

Chapter 2, "A Guide to American Sign Language," covers the major components of ASL grammar. Not a complete grammar of ASL, the guide is intended to help you better understand the structure of the sentences in this book. It is not necessary, however, to understand the grammatical structure before you begin signing those sentences. You may skip over the chapter on grammar and go directly to the sentences and begin signing. As you become more proficient in ASL, you will want to create your own sentences, and then you will need to study the ASL guide. At this stage, the Dictionary/Index will also be helpful to you in locating the signs you want to use in your own expressions.

Chapters 3 through 18 cover the basic topics that occur in the ordinary course of our lives. (The chapter on health also includes some expressions that are needed in emergency situations.) These 16 chapters are self-contained and do not need to be employed in any particular order. You may begin wherever you like, choosing whichever subject you wish, and will be able to proceed without having read the previous chapters. If you are seeking quick access to the rudiments of the language for your first conversations with a deaf person, though, the chapters entitled "Greetings, Salutations, and Everyday Expressions," "Signing and Deafness," and "Getting Acquainted" might be the best ones to begin with.

This book can be used not only as an instant reference manual but also as a study guide should you wish to become fluent in ASL. If you do wish to assimilate the phrases, the most efficient way to use this book is to study one chapter thoroughly, practicing the sentences until you can do them without looking at the pictures. The next step is to use them immediately in conversation. This will help fix them in your memory. To become fluent in ASL, it is important to study and converse in a regular, consistent manner. Do not be afraid of making mistakes, for everyone errs while learning a new language. Deaf people do not expect perfection and usually will cheerfully help you correct your errors.

Sign Labels

To enable us to talk about the signs of ASL each sign has been given a name, or label. We use English words for these labels. In this book the labels appear beneath the picture of the sign. People often confuse the meaning of a sign with its label, but a sign may have several meanings and the label is only one of its meanings. English labels for signs merely provide us with a convenient way of designating which sign we want to talk about or which sign to use.

Let's look at an example. The word *run* has numerous meanings in English. Some of them are:

He *runs* fast.
My nose *runs*.
There's a *run* on the stock market.
She's *running* for office.
He scored a *run*.
Your stocking has a *run* in it.

The sign labeled RUN (Figure 1) could be used only in the first example above, for that is the only meaning of that sign. Each of the other examples requires a different sign.

Figure 1: **RUN**

A sign label does not tell you how a sign may be used to express meanings quite different from the label. Take for example the sign FINISH (Figures 2, 3).

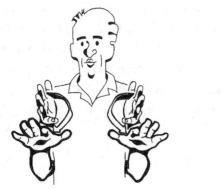

Figure 2: **FINISH**

Figure 3: **FINISH**

The sign phrase EAT FINISH may mean: (1) ate, eaten; (2) already ate, already eaten; (3) did eat; or (4) done eating (Figures 4, 5).

Figure 4: **EAT**

Figure 5: **FINISH**

In this signed sentence, WORK FINISH GO TO HOME (Figures 6–9), the FINISH sign indicates that when one act is over, another follows. This sentence would translate as "After work I am going home," "After work I went home," or "When work is done, I am going home."

Figure 6: **WORK**

Figure 7: **FINISH**

Figure 8: **GO TO**

Figure 9: **HOME**

One form of the FINISH sign by itself can mean "That's enough!" "Stop it!" or "I/She/He did already!" (Figure 10).

The FINISH sign offers an excellent example of the danger of confusing a sign label with the meaning of the sign. Obviously this sign means much more than merely "finish."

Figure 10: **FINISH**

When using the Dictionary/Index at the back of this book to find a sign you want to use, be sure you look for the sign that matches the meaning of the word you have in mind. Do not look just for the English word itself. For example, if you want the sign for "run" in the sense that someone is running for office, you will have to think of "competing," "contesting," or "racing" in order to locate the correct sign (COMPETE, Figure 11).

Figure 11: **COMPETE**

Reading the Drawings

The pictures are to be read from left to right when they are read as a sentence. However, an individual sign may sometimes require more than one picture to illustrate it and will sometimes be read from right to left. Five types of aids are provided to help you know which way to read a drawing and thus form the sign correctly.

Five Aids for Reading the Drawings

The first aid is the use of both *bold* (dark-lined) and *light-lined* drawings. The bold-lined drawings show the final position of the sign. The light-lined drawings show the first and, if necessary, additional positions of the sign. In the sign labeled DELICIOUS (Figure 12), for example, the light-lined drawing shows the middle finger touching the lips. The bold-lined drawing shows the hand turned outward. These are the first and final positions, respectively. Always remember that the bold-lined drawing shows the final position of the sign.

Figure 12: **DELICIOUS**

Figure 13: **DAY**

The second aid is the use of several kinds of *arrows*, which show exactly how the hands move in forming a sign. The sign DAY (Figure 13), for example, is formed by moving the arm from the first position (light-lined) to the final position (bold-lined), following the movement indicated by the arrow.

Repetitive movement is shown by the use of a bent arrow, as in the signs HAPPY (Figure 14) and FOOTBALL (Figure 15). This means you do the same movement twice.

Figure 14: **HAPPY**   *Figure 15:* **FOOTBALL**

Swerving movement is shown by a twisted arrow, as in the sign labeled NEVER (Figure 16).

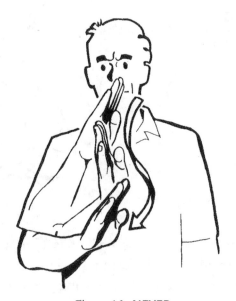

Figure 16: **NEVER**

Circular movement is shown by a circular arrow, as in the signs COFFEE (Figure 17) and GOING (Figure 18).

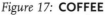

Figure 17: **COFFEE**   *Figure 18:* **GOING**

The arrows in the sign CAR (Figure 19) show the hands repeating a movement, but in opposite directions. The sign looks as if you were steering a car.

In the sign WHICH (Figure 20), the arrows indicate that the hands move alternately. As the left hand goes up, the right hand goes down. Then both hands reverse their directions (left: down; right: up), then they reverse again going in their original directions.

Figure 19: **CAR**   *Figure 20:* **WHICH**

The same thing applies to the sign CONTROL (Figure 21) as does to the WHICH sign, but *numbers*, the third aid, have been added to help you see more clearly where the hands begin and end. When both hands are in their number one positions, the right hand is farther out from the chest than the left. The arrows show that the right hand moves backward, and the left hand moves forward, reversing their positions. The arrows then show that the hands reverse positions again as the hands move to the third position. (Note that both the first and third positions are shown in bold lines since that is the final, as well as the beginning, position. This will occur only rarely, but if in doubt, look at the numbers.) The sign looks as if you are guiding a horse with the reins.

Figure 21: **CONTROL**

The arrows together with the numbers in Figure 22 (HAMBURGER) show a reversal of position here. In the first position the right hand is on top, and in the second position it is on bottom.

Figure 22: **HAMBURGER**

A *broken arrow*, the fourth aid, is shown in Figure 23 (TREES) along with the circular arrows that show how the hand moves from first to final position. The broken arrow means that there may be two or three repetitions of the sign. The sign is repeated (third and fourth positions) only once in the drawing.

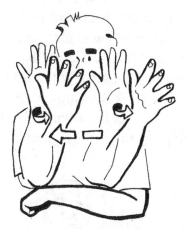

Figure 23: **TREES**

The *squiggles* in Figure 24 (WAIT) are the fifth aid, and they tell you to wriggle the fingers. In the sign for "13" (Figure 25), they tell you to wriggle the index and second finger together, but not the rest of the hand.

Figure 24: **WAIT**   *Figure 25:* **13**

Angle of the Pictures

In most of the drawings the signer is shown facing directly front, but many signs can best be learned by seeing the sign from an angle slightly off center; thus, the signer is sometimes shown facing slightly to his right or to his left. The WANT sign (Figure 26), for instance, would be difficult to read if it were shown straight on, so the signer is shown facing slightly to his right to give you a clearer view of the sign. When you make the sign, however, do not turn to your right, but make it straight toward the person to whom you are signing. In a few of the drawings, such as those for LESSON (Figures 27 and 28), the signer is shown from a rear view, as well as from the front, to help you to see the sign more clearly.

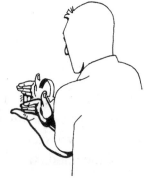

Figure 26: **WANT**   *Figure 27:* **LESSON**   *Figure 28:* **LESSON**
                                                              (rear view)

Labeling of the Drawings

When more than one drawing is required to illustrate how a single sign is made, each sign label is followed by a number. For example, the illustration of the sign AWFUL requires two steps, and these are labeled "AWFUL (1)" and "AWFUL (2)":

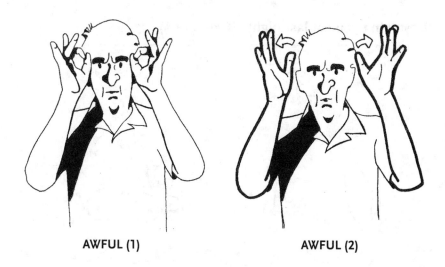

AWFUL (1)   **AWFUL (2)**

When a single concept can be signed in more than one way, several possible signs are shown, and their labels are followed by a letter. For example, the three separate ways to sign BAPTIZE are labeled "BAPTIZE (A)," "BAPTIZE (B)," and "BAPTIZE (C)":

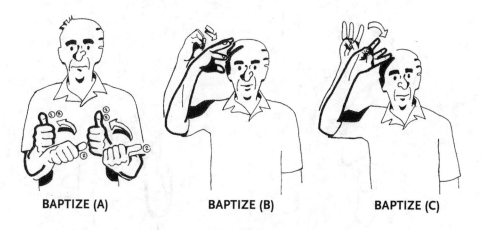

BAPTIZE (A)   **BAPTIZE (B)**   **BAPTIZE (C)**

Sometimes, an entire phrase or sentence can be said in more than one way. In these cases, each sentence, along with its component signs, is shown and indicated with a letter. For example, the sentence "Why didn't you eat last night?" can be signed as "PAST NIGHT YOU EAT NOT WHY" or as "PAST NIGHT WHY YOU EAT NOT":

Why didn't you eat last night? (Example A)

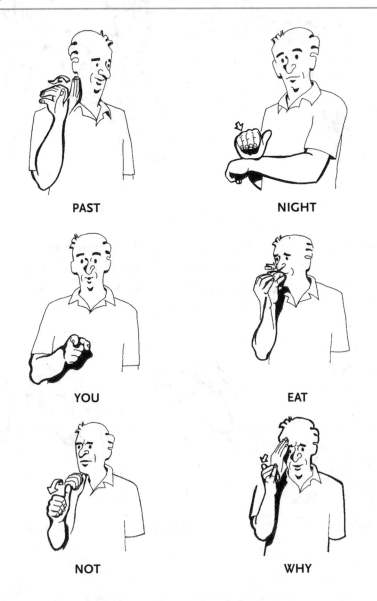

PAST

NIGHT

YOU

EAT

NOT

WHY

Why didn't you eat last night? (Example B)

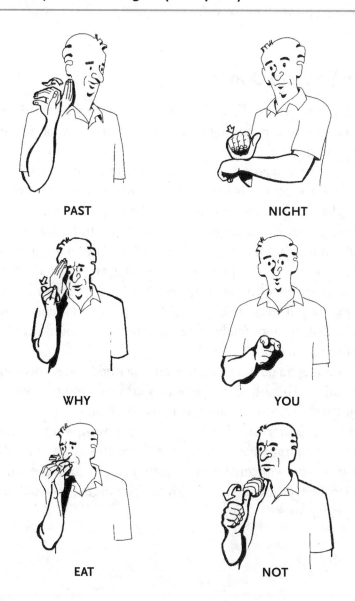

PAST   NIGHT

WHY   YOU

EAT   NOT

Facial Expressions

We have given our cartoon characters various facial expressions to emphasize the importance of facial expressions in ASL. The expressions are by no means the same all the time. The same sign will require different expressions at different times, depending upon the feeling you wish to convey.

Some Dos and Don'ts

Try to avoid any bright light shining directly into the face of the person watching you. Bright lights are to deaf people what noise is to hearing people.

To get a deaf person's attention, gently touch the person on the shoulder. If the person is too far away to touch, wave your arm. Deaf people also get each others' attention by stamping their feet on a wooden floor or by turning a light switch off and on, but it is not recommended that hearing people do this. The manner in which these are done carry subtle meanings that are learned only with years of experience. If you stamped too hard or flashed the light too vigorously, for example, it might mean an emergency situation exists, which, if there really were no emergency, could lead to feelings of consternation.

Make sure you do not stand or sit in the middle of someone else's conversation. This often happens in a crowded room or when two deaf people are seated far apart from each other.

Avoid such nervous behavior as drumming your fingers on a table or tapping your shoe on the floor. If you do such things, the deaf person will constantly turn to look at you to see what you want. Deaf people are extra-sensitive to vibrations, so avoid making unnecessary ones.

2

A Guide to American Sign Language

IN THE UNITED STATES there are several sign systems that should not be confused with American Sign Language (ASL). These systems are ways of putting the English language into a manual-visual form; thus, they are called systems of Manually Coded English (MCEs). They are designed primarily for the purpose of teaching English to deaf children. An MCE uses the same signs that are used in ASL plus many new signs that have been created to serve special functions that do not exist in ASL. In an MCE the signs are arranged in accordance with the rules of English grammar. ASL, on the other hand, is not a way of coding English but rather a language in and of itself. It differs from English in many respects. This book is concerned solely with ASL.

Light, Sight, and Space

Most languages are based entirely on sounds, and herein lies the unique difference between spoken language and ASL. Instead of sound waves in the form of spoken words, ASL uses light waves in the form of signs. ASL is a visual-spatial language. One *sees* ASL, and hearing plays absolutely no part in it. Because of this, ASL consists not only of signs made with the hands but also of facial expressions, head movements, body movements, and an efficient use of the space around the signer. (In ASL the person "speaking" is the *signer*, and the person "listening" is the *watcher, observer,* or *reader*.) ASL is not mime, although mime sometimes is incorporated into the language.

Sight Line

We begin the study of ASL with an understanding of how space is used. Imagine a line extending from the center of the signer's chest, straight out, parallel to the floor. This imaginary line is called the *sight line*. The sight line divides all space into the right or left side.

The Sight Line

The Sight Line (three views)

Whenever the signer turns the body, the sight line moves with it.

One of the most frequently used signs is a simple point with the index finger. When the signer points parallel to the sight line toward the watcher, it means "you." When the signer points to his or her own chest, it means "I" or "me." When the signer points to the right or the left of the sight line, it means "he," "she," or "it."

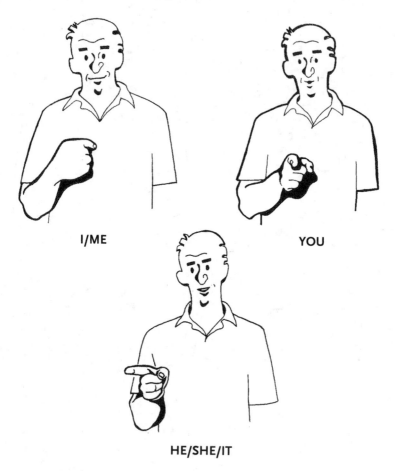

I/ME   YOU

HE/SHE/IT

Placement of Signs

People, places, objects, and events may be established or placed to the right and left of the sight line. Once this is done, the signer merely points to that space when reference to it is made. For example, as in the phrase depicted here, suppose the signer tells the watcher, "I saw your father yesterday. He was driving a new car."

I saw your father yesterday. He was driving a new car.

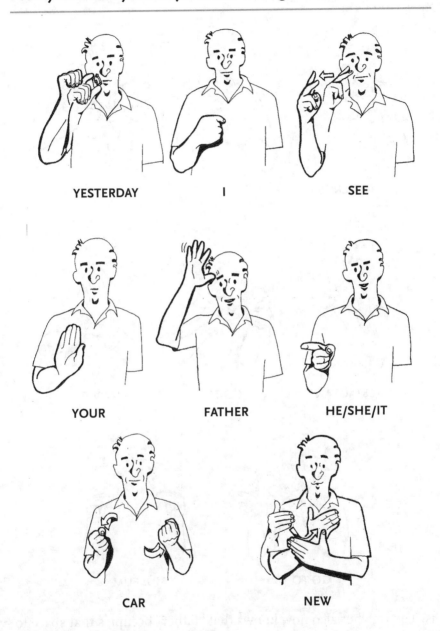

YESTERDAY   I   SEE

YOUR   FATHER   HE/SHE/IT

CAR   NEW

The signer makes the sign for "see" toward the right (or toward the left, if the signer is left-handed). This movement tells the watcher that the signer is about to say something about someone. Then the signer signs "father," and that tells the watcher who the someone

Yesterday I went to a restaurant, a movie, and a museum.

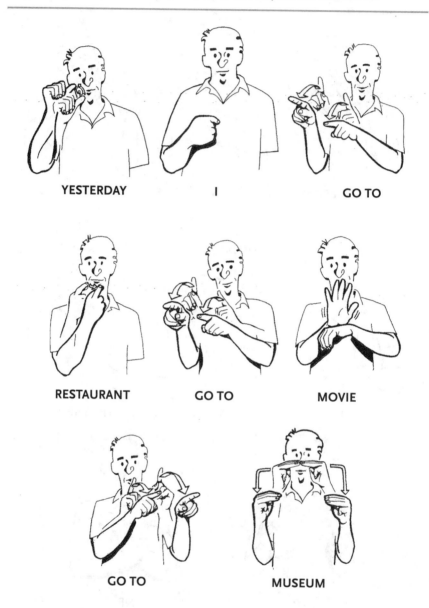

is. The watcher also now knows that "father" occupies that space to the right of the sight line because the SEE sign moved toward that space. The signer may now point right, and it means "he," and it will continue to mean "he" (father) until the signer places someone or something else in that space.

Placement of more than one person, place, or object in the same space at the same time may not be done, but placement in other spaces at the same time may be done.

For example, the signer may say, "Yesterday I went to a restaurant, a movie, and a museum." The three places are set up in three different spaces. Notice that the restaurant is nearer the signer, and the movie is farther out. Both may be to the right of the sight line, but they occupy slightly different spaces.

Avoid placing persons on the sight line itself. This space, with some exceptions, is reserved for the watcher. Any signs that move on or along the sight line have to do with the watcher, and no one else may occupy this area. An exception to this rule is illustrated by the following example:

I have a book. It is interesting.

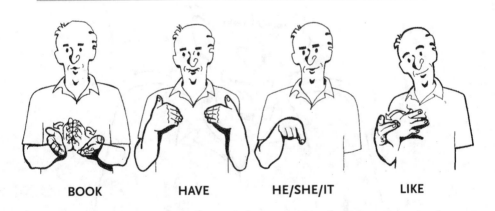

| BOOK | HAVE | HE/SHE/IT | LIKE |

The signer first establishes the book, then points to it. When placing things on the sight line that have no reference to the watcher, place them near the signer and be sure to point to that space.

Facial Expressions

In a spoken language, the rise and fall of the voice adds meaning to the words spoken. The various ways one can say "I love you" illustrate the importance of vocal inflection. The characteristic rising of the voice toward the end of a question is another example. In ASL, the face has these duties and supplies additional subtleties and nuances of meaning. Signs have meanings in and of themselves, just as words do, but these meanings are altered, shaped, enriched, and amplified by facial expressions. A face that is devoid of expression is to a deaf person the equivalent of a monotone speaker—boring and difficult to follow.

Facial expressions in ASL are especially important when asking questions. In general, when one asks a *wh-* sign question (who, what, why, where, when, which, and how) the eyebrows usually go downward.

All other questions usually cause the eyebrows to move upward.

These are not rigid rules, and you may sometimes see something different, but these rules do generally apply. That the eyebrows will move up or down, however, is a certainty when asking questions.

The signer must learn to be expressive with the eyes and mouth as well as with the eyebrows. The eyes will open wide or squint to narrow slits; the mouth will open and close; the lips will purse and stretch; the cheeks will puff out; and even the tongue will sometimes protrude.

Body Language

Body language is an essential element of ASL. Information is communicated not only by the face but also by the head, shoulders, torso, legs, and feet. The head may tilt forward, back, or to the side, especially when questions are asked.

The shoulders may shrug; the body may bend forward and back-ward and twist.

The incorporation of the whole body into the expression of sign language is absolutely required for clear, understandable communication. It is possible, of course, to overdo the matter, but it is better to err on the side of doing too much than too little. Deaf people are often described as animated, alive, vibrant, etc. This is due to their mastery of body language. For successful communication, you must do likewise.

For additional practice in facial expressions, body language, and the use of the hands to express ideas and convey information, I suggest the book and videotapes produced by Gilbert Eastman entitled *From Mime to Sign.*

Past, Present, and Future

One of the most difficult tasks in learning a new language is conjugating verbs in their various tenses. The struggle with regular and irregular verbs tries the student's patience to the utmost. It is, therefore, a pleasure to inform you that such is not the case with ASL. Learning to place actions in the past or future is comparatively simple.

No tenses are incorporated in the signs themselves. Tense is conveyed by using signs that tell when an action takes place, and these particular signs are called *time indicators*. In English, for example, one may say, "I saw you." In ASL, the sign SEE is always made the same way whether it means "see," "sees," "seeing," "saw," or "seen":

SEE

In order to sign the equivalent of "I saw you," it is necessary to use a time indicator. One may use signs that will place the event in a specific time, such as "yesterday," "last night," or "this morning."

Yesterday, I saw.

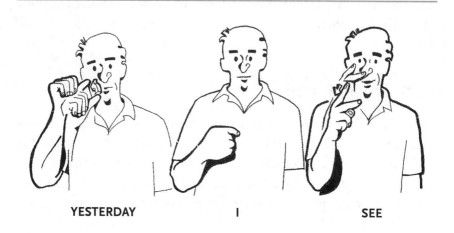

YESTERDAY   I   SEE

Last night, I saw.

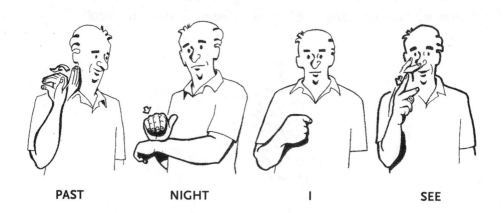

PAST   NIGHT   I   SEE

This morning, I saw.

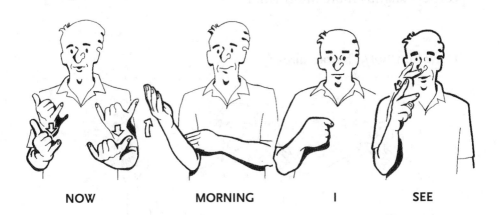

NOW	**MORNING**	**I**	**SEE**

One may also use the FINISH sign to indicate no specific time, simply the past:

I saw.

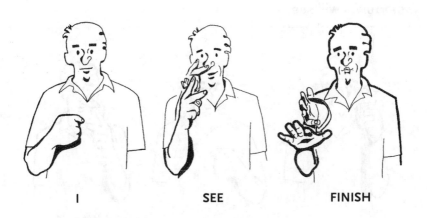

I	**SEE**	**FINISH**

The PAST sign may be used instead of the FINISH sign, which conveys slightly more information.

I saw him/her/it before already.

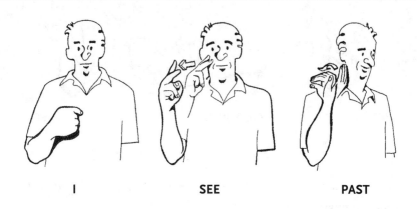

| I | SEE | PAST |

The use of a time indicator also applies to the future tense.

Tomorrow, I will see.

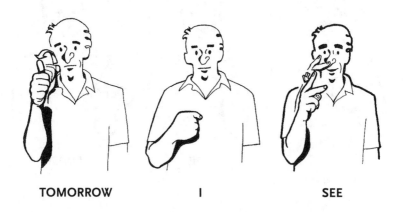

| TOMORROW | I | SEE |

Next week, I will see.

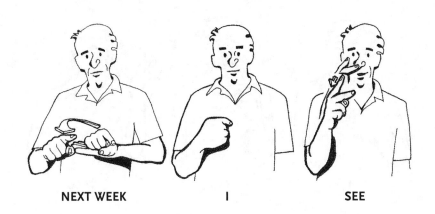

NEXT WEEK I SEE

Tonight, I will see.

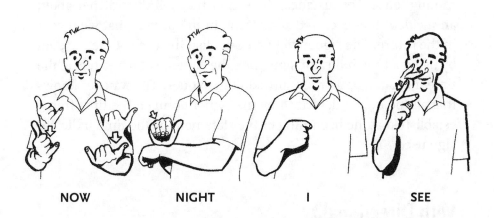

NOW NIGHT I SEE

The previous phrases illustrate placing the event in a specific future time. For a nonspecific future time, use the WILL sign.

I will see.

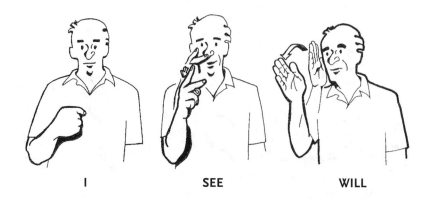

| I | SEE | WILL |

Notice that nonspecific time indicators such as FINISH and WILL usually follow the verb; however, they may come before the verb as well. Specific time indicators, on the other hand, always come at the beginning of a statement.

Context is used a great deal in ASL when establishing or determining tense. For instance, the signer may tell the watcher about an incident that occurred some time in the past or that will occur in the future. The signer will first establish the time of the incident by using a time indicator sign; then the signer will never repeat the time indicator sign or use any additional ones. The watcher knows that all the events described by the signer occur in the time frame established at the beginning of the statement by the time indicator sign used.

Verb Directionality

Verbs in ASL fall into three categories: nondirectional verbs, one-directional verbs, and multi-directional verbs. Movement in verb signs may express who is performing an action (the subject) and to whom the action is directed (the direct object). This quality of movement is called verb directionality.

The nondirectional verbs do not express either subject or direct object; therefore, these two things (subject and direct object nouns and pronouns) must be supplied.

I love you.

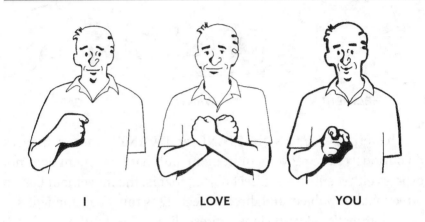

| I | LOVE | YOU |

I understand mother.

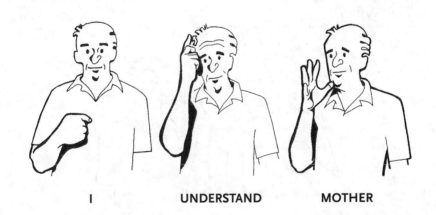

| I | UNDERSTAND | MOTHER |

She wants a car.

HE/SHE/IT   WANT   CAR

The verbs LOVE, UNDERSTAND, and WANT in these sentences do obviously have movement in them, but that movement does not express either subject or direct object; that is, the movement has no directionality. Subject and direct object signs must be supplied.

One-directional verb signs express direct object but not subject, as in these sentences:

I see him/her/it.

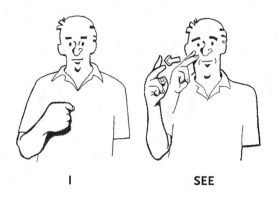

I   SEE

You tell him/her.

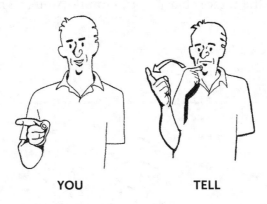

YOU   TELL

She follows him/her/it.

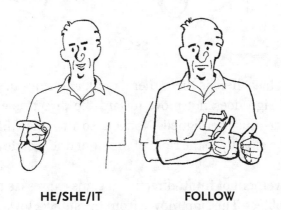

HE/SHE/IT   FOLLOW

One-directional verbs move toward the direct object; thus, a noun or pronoun is not required. The exception to this rule occurs when the signer is the direct object. For example, "You see me" must be signed:

You see me.

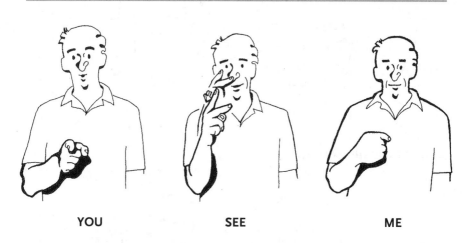

| YOU | SEE | ME |

The direct object here is the signer ("me"), and since the movement of the SEE sign does not move toward the direct object, then the direct object must be signed. Notice also that the SEE sign does indeed move slightly to the right of the sight line, not directly toward the watcher.

The movement of multi-directional signs expresses both subject and direct object. The sign moves from the subject toward the direct object; thus, neither the subject nor direct object is signed.

I help you.

HELP

In the following illustration, the body is faced to your left to give you a better view of how the sign is made, but the sign itself goes along the sight line from the signer to the watcher.

He helps me.   ## He helps her.

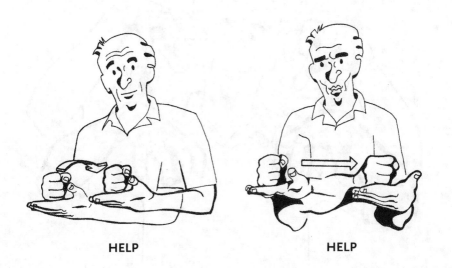

HELP   **HELP**

The movement from a space normally implies that whoever occupies that space is the subject. The movement toward a space normally implies that whoever occupies that space is the direct object.

To Be or Not to Be

Many sentences in English require some form of the "to be" verb. Examples of such sentences include "I am fine," "You are tired," "Where is Joe?" and "They were not here." There is no "to be" verb in ASL. The above examples are signed, "I FINE," "YOU TIRED," "WHERE JOE?" and "THEY NOT HERE." Statements such as "It is raining," "The flower is growing," and "The train is late" are signed:

It is raining.

RAIN

The flower is growing.

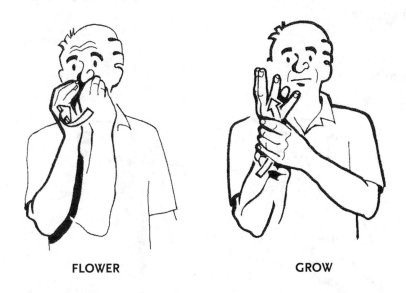

FLOWER GROW

The train is late.

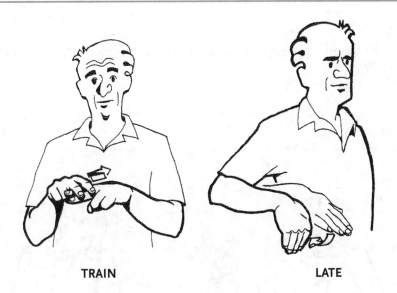

TRAIN LATE

When the signer wishes to stress or emphasize statements, then the TRUE sign is used. The following statement means simply that "I am sick":

I am sick.

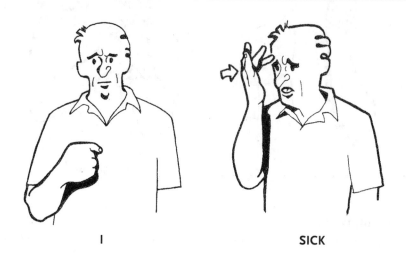

I   SICK

The following statement means that "I am really sick," or "I am very sick":

I am really sick.

I   TRUE   SICK

Do not confuse the use of the TRUE sign as a sign of stress and emphasis with a form of the "to be" verb in English.

The TRUE sign also means *true, truly, real, really, sure, surely, certainly, indeed,* and *actually.* When used alone with a questioning expression, the TRUE sign means "Is that so?" or "Are you sure?"

Words Versus Signs

A word stands for a concept or an idea. If someone says "tree," you understand immediately because you have in your mind the concept of tree. The same applies to signs. If the signer signs TREE, the watcher understands it immediately without having to think the word *tree.* In other words, a sign stands for an idea or concept; it does not stand for a word.

When you form statements in ASL, do not try to find a sign for every word in the English statement. Languages do not work that way. (For example, in English one says, "I am hungry," but in Spanish and French one says, "I have hunger." In ASL one says, "I hunger.") First get clearly in mind the ideas you want to communicate, forget the words, and then find the appropriate signs to express the ideas.

Making Statements

Language is made up of utterances or statements. In spoken languages the statements consist of words, but in ASL the statements consist of signs and fingerspelling. There are two kinds of statements, those that ask questions and those that do not ask questions. Let's look at how these statements are formed in ASL.

Statements That Ask Questions

1. Yes/No Questions. These are such questions as, "Are you hungry?" and "Do you want to go to the movies?" This type of question is usually accompanied by the types of head tilts shown on pages 27 and 28 and by raised eyebrows as shown on page 25. The eyebrows are not *always* raised, but generally they are.

Are you hungry?

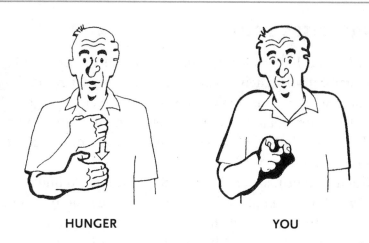

HUNGER   YOU

Do you want to go to the movies?

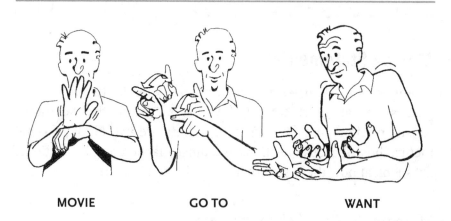

MOVIE   GO TO   WANT

2. Wh- Sign Questions. These are the questions that use *who*, *what*, *why*, *where*, *when*, *which*, and *how*, and they require more than a yes/no answer. These questions are also accompanied by one of the head tilts shown on pages 27 and 28 and by lowered eyebrows as shown on page 24. Again, the eyebrows may not always be lowered, but generally they are.

WHO

WHAT SHRUG

WHAT

WHY

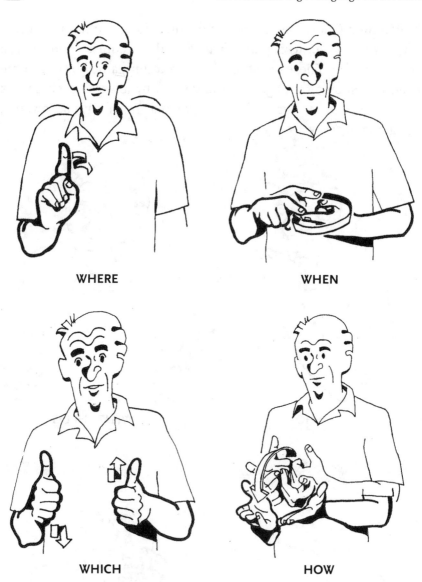

WHERE

WHEN

WHICH

HOW

The *wh-* sign may come at the beginning or at the end of a question, or it may appear in both places. If you wish to emphasize a question, place it at the end.

Why didn't you eat last night? (Example A)

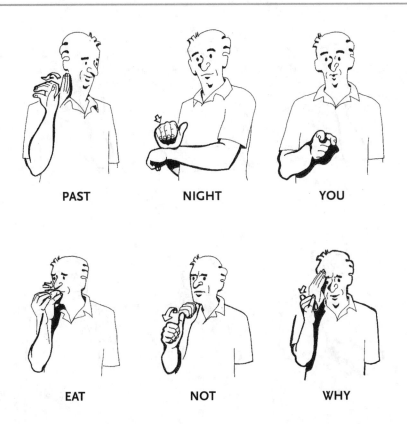

PAST   NIGHT   YOU

EAT   NOT   WHY

Why didn't you eat last night? (Example B)

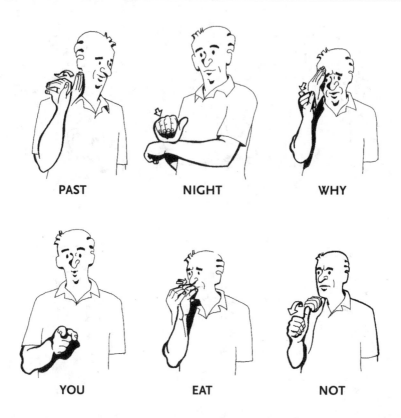

PAST NIGHT WHY

YOU EAT NOT

Which do you want, coffee or tea? (Example A)

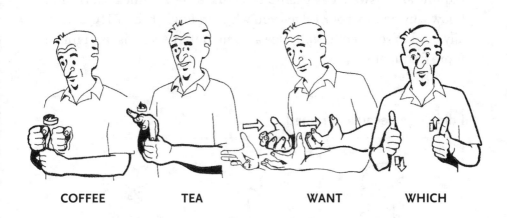

COFFEE   TEA   WANT   WHICH

Which do you want, coffee or tea? (Example B)

WANT   WHICH   COFFEE   TEA

Naturally the signer makes a questioning facial expression when using these *wh-* sign questions.

Do not use a *wh-* sign in statements that do not ask questions. In English, for example, we may make such statements as, "When I say 'frog,' jump!" or "Where there is smoke there is fire." In these statements the *wh-* word does not ask a question; therefore, *wh-* signs are not used. A different way of making the statement is used.

3. Rhetorical Questions (RHQ). This type of question does not require an answer. For example, "What's in a name?" and "You know why he won't go? I'll tell you why." In English, an RHQ is usually used to set off or emphasize a point, but in ASL it is used much more frequently.

I didn't go because it rained.

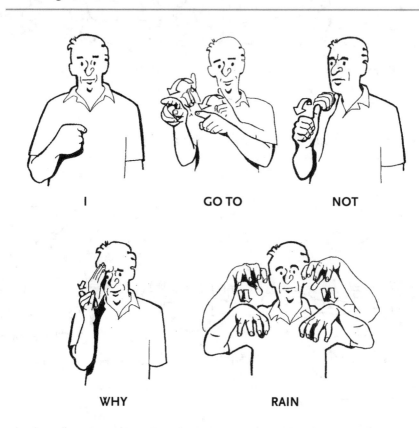

I　　　　　GO TO　　　　　NOT

WHY　　　　　RAIN

I flew./I went by airplane.

I	GO TO

HOW	AIRPLANE

4. Negative Questions. These are questions such as "Don't you understand?" or "Why didn't you tell me?" Ask them the same way you would a yes/no or a *wh-* sign question, but put in some form of negation. Usually you just shake your head as you ask the question, but you may add a sign of negation as well.

Why didn't you tell me?

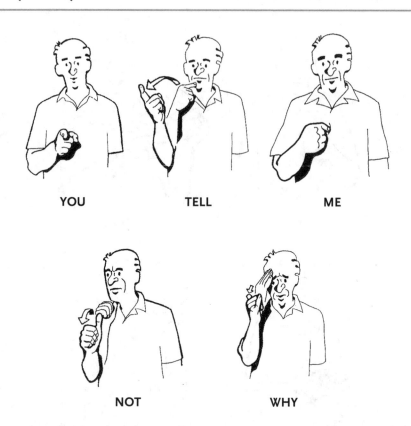

YOU   TELL   ME

NOT   WHY

Statements That Do Not Ask Questions

1. Simple Statements. These are called "simple" because they are signed exactly the way they are spoken in English. Some examples are "I know you," "You tell me," "He loves you," "She likes movies." They have what is called the subject-verb-object arrangement.

I know you.

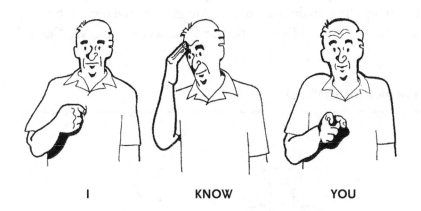

| I | KNOW | YOU |

You tell me.

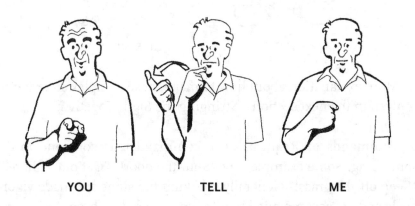

| YOU | TELL | ME |

She likes movies.

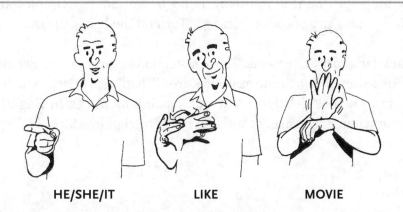

| HE/SHE/IT | LIKE | MOVIE |

2. Complex Statements. These are called "complex" because they involve two objects and are *not* signed exactly the way they are spoken in English. In the statement "You give me the book," the subject is "you," the first object is "me," and the second object is "book."

You give me the book.

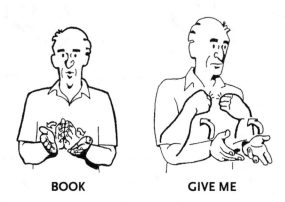

BOOK   GIVE ME

More explanation about how to make these complex statements is given in the next section, "Stringing the Signs Together."

3. Commands or Requests. The command tells someone to do something. Some examples are "Shut the door!" "Get out of here!" "Keep off the grass!" Generally speaking the signs are made vigorously and are accompanied by a frown (lowered eyebrows).

The request differs from the command only in that it is followed by the sign PLEASE and there is no frown. Some examples are "Bring me a cup of coffee, please," "Turn off the lights, please."

4. Exclamatory Statements. These statements express a strong reaction to something. Some examples are "What!" (surprise), "Ouch!" (pain), "Yahoo!" (elation), "Far out!" (admiration). As in English, these statements usually consist of only one sign in ASL.

Stringing the Signs Together

The fascinating part of any language is learning how to put the words together correctly to make a statement. The way words are strung together is the syntax of a language. Except for simple statements, commands, requests, and exclamatory statements, ASL differs considerably from English in syntax.

First, we need to deal with the concept of topicalization, which means that a statement begins with a topic. The topic may be a person, a thing, an action, or an event. In the example used earlier, "You give me the book," the topic is *the book*. If we topicalize this statement in English, it comes out "The book, you give it to me." Although there is nothing wrong with saying it this way, it sounds awkward to our ears because we are not used to topicalizing in English. The statement "Do you see the woman in the red hat?" if topicalized, comes out "The woman in the red hat, do you see her?" The topic here is *the woman*, a person. "I enjoy going for long walks" comes out "Going for long walks, I enjoy them." Here the topic is *going for long walks*, an activity. "It was a long and difficult test" comes out "The test, it was long and difficult." The topic is *the test*, an event.

The topic of a statement is always followed by the comment. In the above examples, the comments are *you give it to me, in the red hat, I enjoy them,* and *it was long and difficult.*

Topic-Comment Statements

To topicalize a statement in ASL, you must first identify the topic and the comment. Because this is something you are not used to doing, it may appear difficult, but with practice it becomes easier. Topic-comment statements fall into one of several categories, which makes them easier to identify. Let's look at these categories.

1. Descriptive Statements. In these statements the topic is described and the description is the comment. An example is "I bought a new, red car." The topic is *car*, the comment is *new, red, I bought.* In ASL, the color of an object usually takes precedence over other qualities, so the comment would be *red, new, I bought*. The signed statement comes out CAR RED NEW BUY ME. (We will talk more later about the pronoun *me* coming after the verb *buy*.)

I bought a new red car.

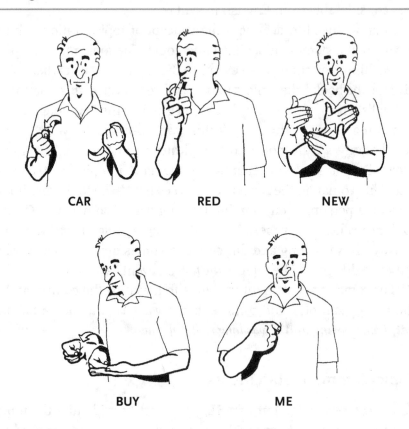

CAR   RED   NEW

BUY   ME

In the statement "I really enjoyed living in that big old house," the topic is *house* and the comment is *big, old, I really enjoyed living there*. In ASL, the size of an object generally comes first, and the emotional reaction comes last (more about this later, too). The statement is signed HOUSE BIG OLD LIVE THERE ENJOY ME TRUE.

I really enjoyed living in that big old house.

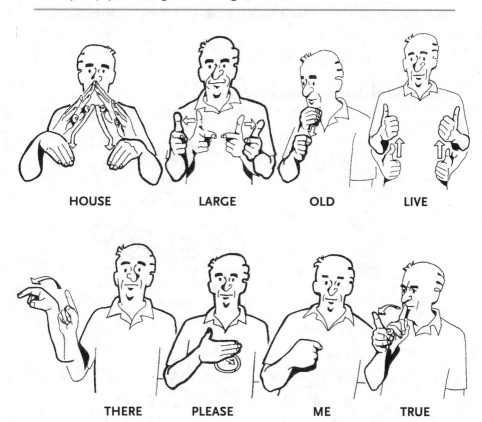

HOUSE LARGE OLD LIVE

THERE PLEASE ME TRUE

2. Cause and Effect or Stimulus-Response Statements. In real life, you cannot have an effect without first having a cause, or a response without first having a stimulus. I cannot, for example, scream before a safe falls out of the sky and lands a few feet from me. Neither could I yell "Ouch!" before stubbing my toe on a chair leg. The safe (the cause) must fall first, and the stubbing of my toe (the stimulus) must happen first. The cause/stimulus in these kinds of statements is the topic, the effect/response is the comment.

In the statement "I'm scared of thunder and lightning," the cause/stimulus is *thunder and lightning,* and the effect/response is *scared of.*

I'm scared of thunder and lightning.

LIGHTNING   SHAKE

SCARE   I

In the statement "I felt better after I took the medicine," the cause/stimulus is *took the medicine,* and the effect/response is *felt better.*

I felt better after I took the medicine.

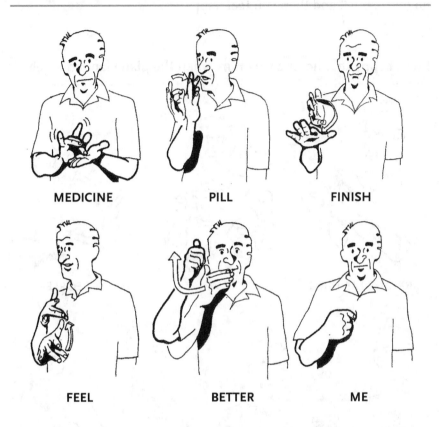

MEDICINE	PILL	FINISH
FEEL	BETTER	ME

3. Statements That Require Real-Time Sequencing. "Real-time sequencing" means that the events in a statement must be arranged in the chronological order in which they occurred in real life, another way of saying that the cause/stimulus must come before the effect/response.

In the statement "I was happy that no one was hurt when the plane landed safely," the events are not in chronological order. Rearranged to conform to real-time sequencing, the statement reads, "When the plane landed safely and no one was hurt, I was happy." Picture the scene in your mind as if you were watching it happen.

First you see the plane land, then you see everyone get out and that no one is hurt, and then you feel happy.

I was happy that no one was hurt when the plane landed safely.

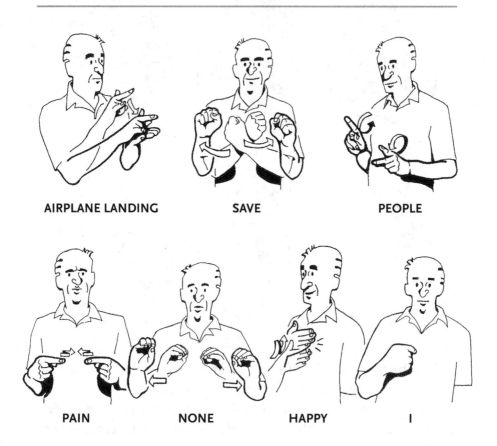

AIRPLANE LANDING   SAVE   PEOPLE

PAIN   NONE   HAPPY   I

4. Statements That Move from General to Specific. These statements require that you visualize the whole scene, just as you did with the airplane, but this time you move from the large to the small. An example is "There's an old man in the white house on that farm."

First see the whole picture of a farm with a white house on it; then move in closer to see an old man in the house.

There's an old man in the white house on that farm.

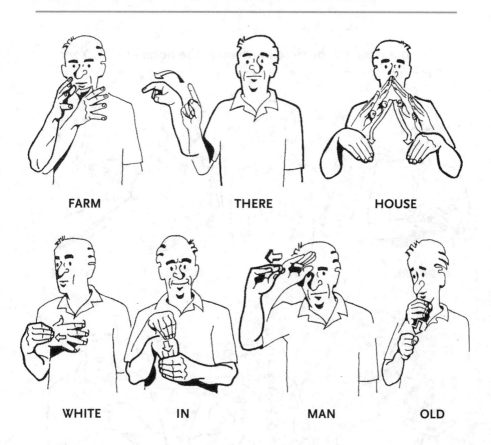

FARM   THERE   HOUSE

WHITE   IN   MAN   OLD

Another example is "I was exhausted by the time I arrived at the hotel in New York." Start with the largest thing, "New York"; then work down to the next largest thing, "hotel." The next largest thing after "hotel" is "I." See yourself arriving at the hotel and then feeling exhausted.

I was exhausted by the time I arrived at the hotel in New York.

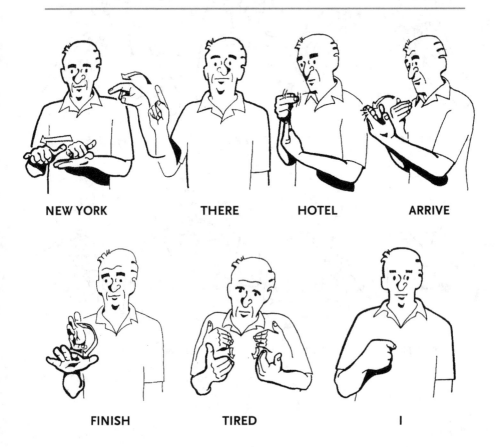

NEW YORK   THERE   HOTEL   ARRIVE

FINISH   TIRED   I

Your success in putting the signs in the correct order, as you probably can tell by now, lies in your ability to imagine, to visualize a scene. ASL is, after all, a visual language, so you must develop this skill.

Pronouns

Pronoun signs tend to come before verbs, at the end of statements, and often in both positions. As a rule, they tend to appear at the end of a statement more often than at the beginning, but this rule is honored as much in the breaking as in the keeping of it. As a result, you will not be wrong if you put it in either or both places.

All the pronouns may be expressed by just three hand shapes. The first group is made up of the pointing pronouns. Simply point to get: *I, me, you, he, she, him, her, it.*

The second group is the possessive pronouns:

MY   HIS/HER/ITS

YOUR   OUR

The third group is the self pronouns:

Third person plural pronouns move in a very small arc:

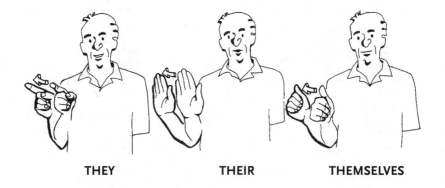

First and second person singular pointing pronouns tend to come at the end of a statement:

I want to go to the movie.

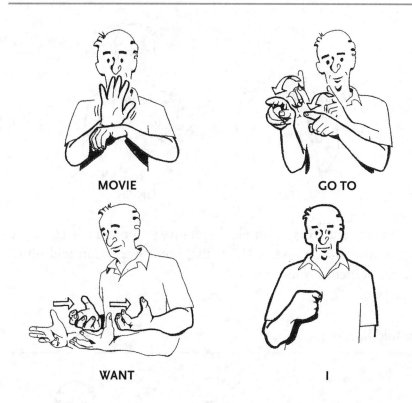

MOVIE

GO TO

WANT

I

Sometimes the first and second person singular point pronoun is dropped entirely, especially in questions:

Do you like to watch TV?

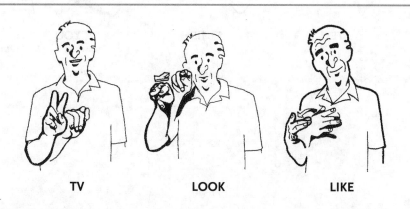

TV

LOOK

LIKE

I told him/her.

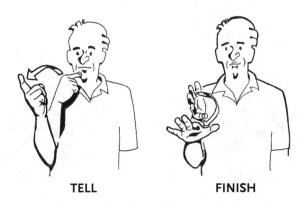

TELL   FINISH

The statement above is a simple declarative statement of fact, so you may assume the subject is "I." If the intent were "You told him," then the sentence would be:

You told him/her.

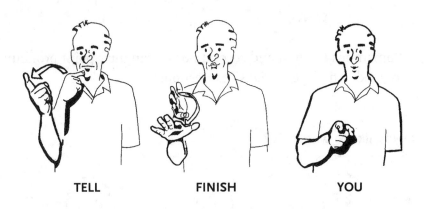

TELL   FINISH   YOU

The second person singular pointing pronoun is usually dropped in questions, as here:

Did you tell him/her?

TELL   FINISH

If the intent here were "Did I tell him?" then it would be signed:

Did I tell him/her?

TELL   FINISH   I

Command forms rarely use pronouns:

Tell him/her!

TELL

Negation

The most common way to negate a statement in ASL is to shake the head while you are making a sign. For example, to say "I do not understand," shake your head as you sign "I understand." The shaking of the head negates the statement so that it means "I do not understand." This practice applies to nearly all signs, including negative signs themselves. If the signer adds NOT in the above statement, and simultaneously shakes the head, the negation is emphasized. We know that English grammar does not permit double negatives, but in Spanish one may say "Yo no sé nada," which literally means "I not know nothing." Spanish here may be compared to ASL, where one may sign UNDERSTAND NOTHING while shaking the head, thus creating a double negative.

In general, a negative sign follows the thing it negates. It may also come before, and it may come both before and after. For emphasis, however, it always follows the thing it negates. The latter is especially true in negative commands.

She tells me nothing.

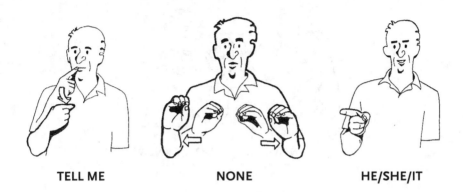

| TELL ME | NONE | HE/SHE/IT |

I didn't tell him.

| TELL | NOT | I |

You can't go.

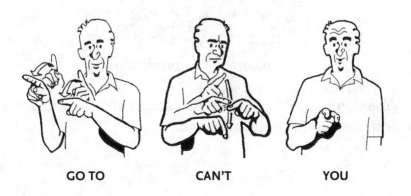

| GO TO | CAN'T | YOU |

Many signs have negation built into them:

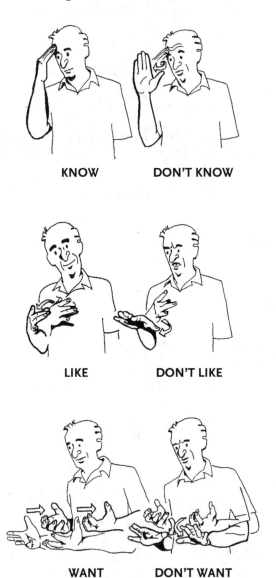

| KNOW | DON'T KNOW |

| LIKE | DON'T LIKE |

| WANT | DON'T WANT |

The signer should always shake the head while simultaneously making the negative form of the sign.

More Final Signs

In addition to the final position of the pronoun, there are other signs that tend to appear in the final position. For example,

I want to go to the movies tomorrow.

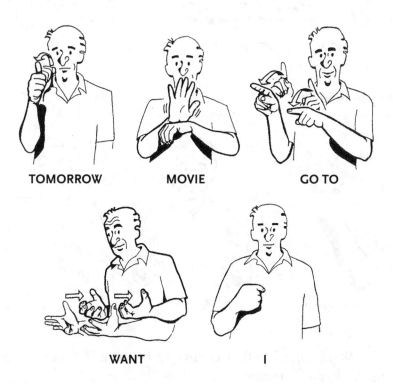

TOMORROW   MOVIE   GO TO

WANT   I

The WANT sign comes after the verb because it belongs to a class of signs that expresses obligation, necessity, feelings, moods, states of mind, and intentions. Some other signs in this class are HOPE, CAN, MUST, and WILL. They do not always follow the verb, sometimes they precede it, and often they appear both before and after the verb.

I hope it clears up this afternoon.

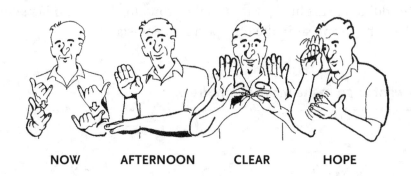

NOW   AFTERNOON   CLEAR   HOPE

Can you read lips?

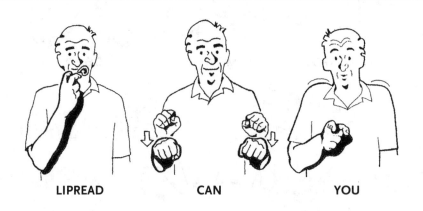

LIPREAD   CAN   YOU

The WILL sign is often confusing because it expresses both future tense and intention.

I will never tell.

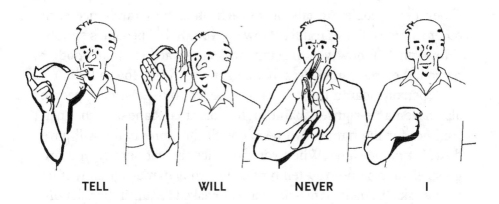

TELL	WILL	NEVER	I

A final word about signs in the final position is that if you want to emphasize something, put it at or near the end of the statement. The last thing seen is the thing best remembered.

Plurals

Often signs are repeated or moved in a way that shows plurality.

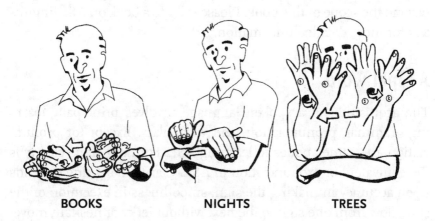

BOOKS	NIGHTS	TREES

When a sign does not lend itself to this kind of repetition or pluralizing movement, then signers use such signs as MANY, FEW, and SOME, or they use specific numbers such as NINE or FIFTY.

Names and Titles

When deaf people are talking to each other they rarely use each other's names. For example, "How are you, Bob?" becomes simply, "How you?" If, however, the signer asks the watcher about another person, then the signer uses that person's name. ("How is Bob?")

A person's name must be fingerspelled, but most deaf people also have name-signs. A name-sign is one that stands for that person, not for the name. Two people with the same name will have different name-signs. When you first meet a deaf person, you fingerspell your name. You tell him or her your name-sign only if he or she asks. Usually name-signs are not asked for until the relationship develops beyond that of a casual acquaintance.

Titles such as "Mrs.," "Dr.," and "Rev." are fingerspelled and used only when the person is being introduced. You never use them when you are talking directly to the person. "How are you, Dr. Smith?" becomes simply "How you?"

Articles

A discussion of articles (*a, an, the*) in American Sign Language is beyond the scope of this book. Please refer to a book on ASL linguistics for more detailed information.

A Final Word

The acquisition of a spoken language involves principally learning grammar, pronunciation, and vocabulary. Except for pronunciation, the same applies to learning ASL. Forming signs clearly is the equivalent of pronunciation in ASL. Clarity in signing depends upon accuracy in making the sign, smoothness in execution of the sign, flow from one sign to the next without jerky or hesitant movements, the use of facial expressions, the use of head and body movements, and the proper use of space. The only way to develop these is through using the language with deaf people. They will correct you when you err, and by watching them carefully you will correct and fine-tune yourself.

3

Greetings, Salutations, and Everyday Expressions

Hello.

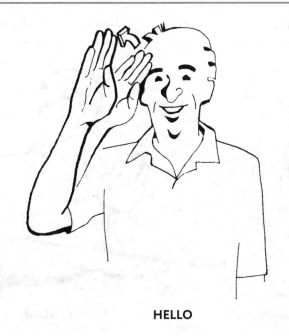

HELLO

Good morning.

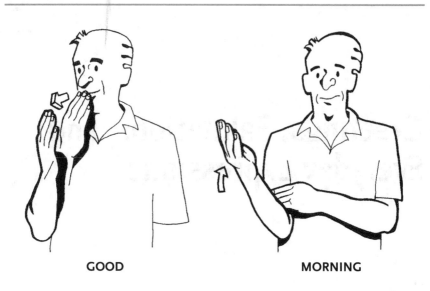

GOOD

MORNING

Good afternoon.

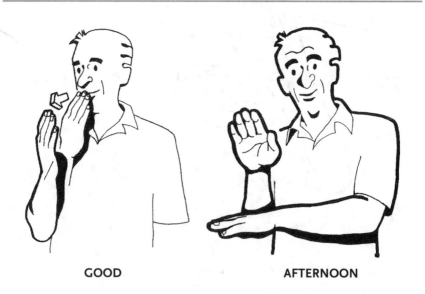

GOOD

AFTERNOON

Good night.

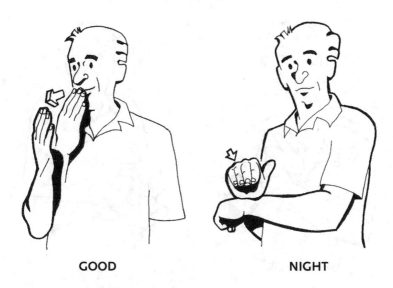

GOOD NIGHT

How are you?

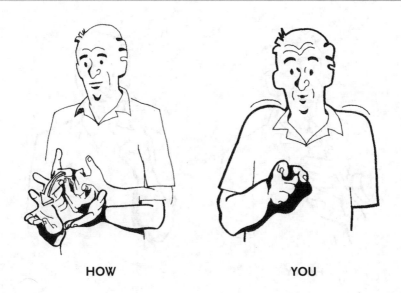

HOW YOU

How have you been?

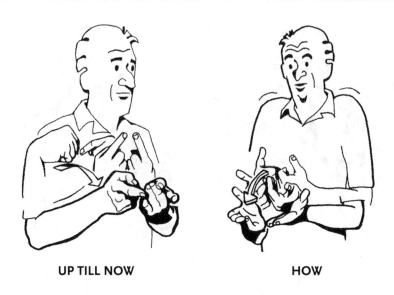

UP TILL NOW   HOW

I'm glad to see you.

HAPPY   SEE

See you later.

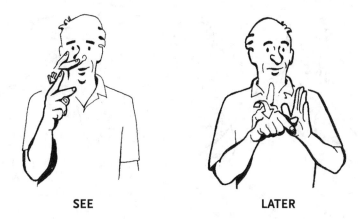

SEE   LATER

Good-bye.

GOOD-BYE

I feel fine.

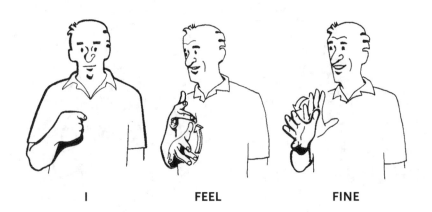

| I | FEEL | FINE |

Additional vocabulary

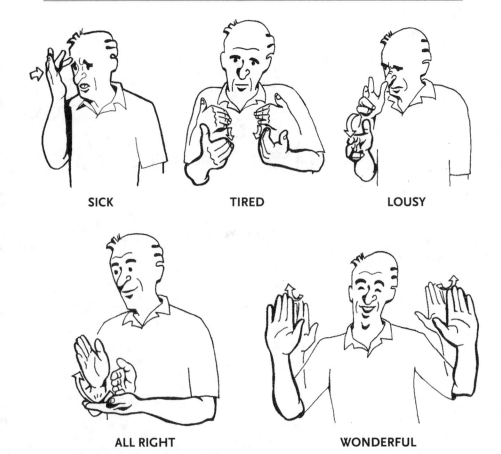

| SICK | TIRED | LOUSY |

| ALL RIGHT | WONDERFUL |

I haven't seen you for a long time. (Example A)

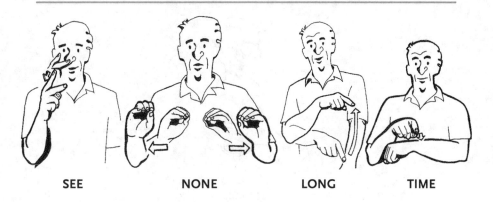

SEE   NONE   LONG   TIME

I haven't seen you for a long time. (Example B)

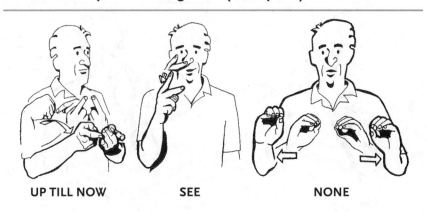

UP TILL NOW   SEE   NONE

Thank you.

GOOD

Please.

PLEASE

No, thank you.

NO

GOOD

Pardon me.

EXCUSE

Where is the restroom?

TOILET

WHERE

Close the door.

CLOSE DOOR

Open the door.

OPEN DOOR

Close the window.

CLOSE WINDOW

Open the window.

OPEN WINDOW

Do you like to watch TV?

TV   LOOK   LIKE

Do you want to go to the movies?

MOVIE   GO TO   WANT

What's your phone number?

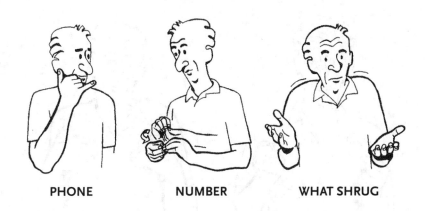

PHONE   NUMBER   WHAT SHRUG

Do you have a TTY?

Note: The TTY or TDD is a device that permits one to type messages back and forth over the telephone.

T-T-Y   HAVE

Do you have a car?

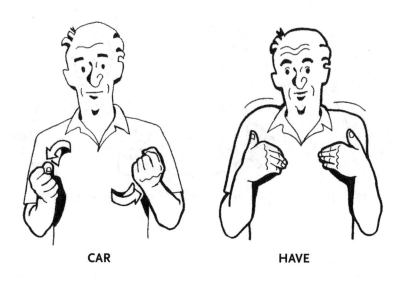

CAR   HAVE

May I go with you?

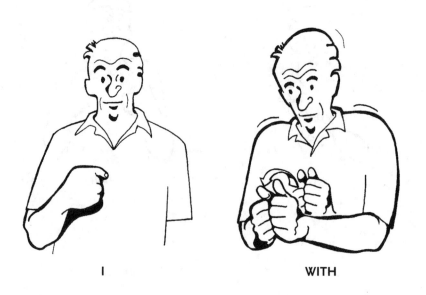

I   WITH

Have a seat, please.

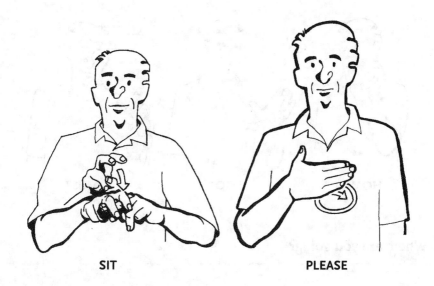

SIT   PLEASE

What time is it?

TIME

I have to go home.

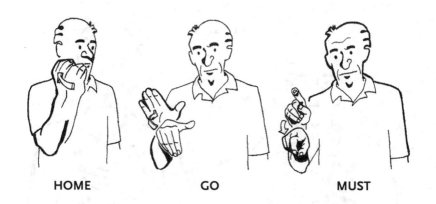

HOME GO MUST

Where are you going?

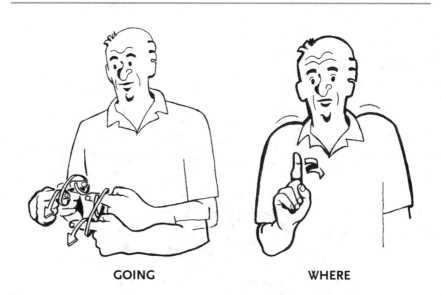

GOING WHERE

I'm sorry.

SORRY

Have a nice Thanksgiving.

HAVE   **NICE**   **THANKSGIVING (1)**   **THANKSGIVING (2)**

Merry Christmas.

Note: For Christmas Eve, the word *Eve* is fingerspelled.

HAPPY **CHRISTMAS**

Happy Hanukkah.

HAPPY **HANUKKAH**

Happy New Year.

Note: For New Year's Eve, the word *Eve* is fingerspelled.

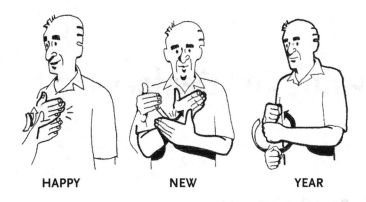

| HAPPY | NEW | YEAR |

Happy birthday.

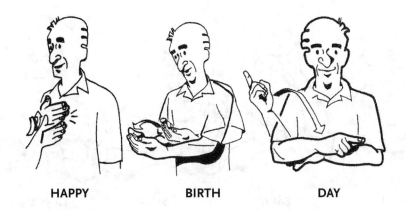

| HAPPY | BIRTH | DAY |

4

Signing and Deafness

I'm learning sign language.

The sign LANGUAGE is usually not signed in this expression, so that it reads literally: "I am learning to sign."

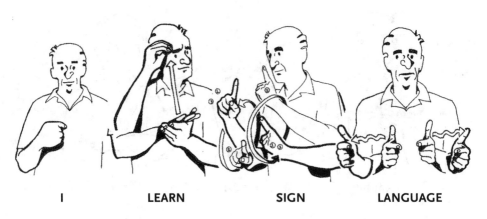

| I | LEARN | SIGN | LANGUAGE |

Sign slowly, please.

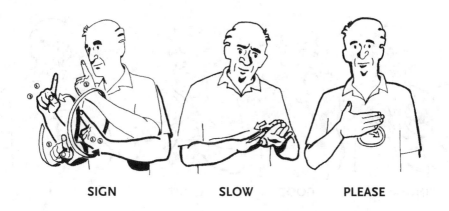

SIGN	SLOW	PLEASE

Please repeat.

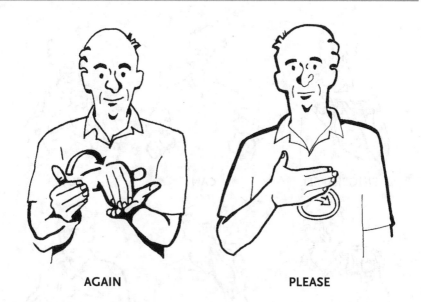

AGAIN	PLEASE

I can't fingerspell well.

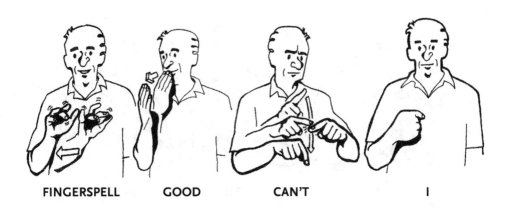

FINGERSPELL   GOOD   CAN'T   I

I can fingerspell, but I can't read it well.

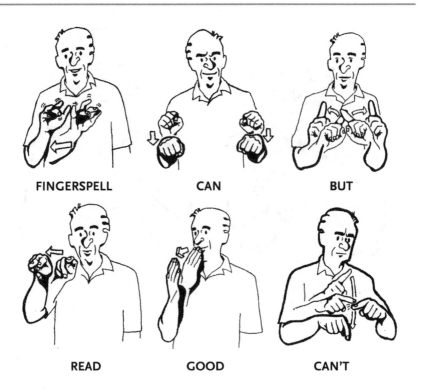

FINGERSPELL   CAN   BUT

READ   GOOD   CAN'T

You sign fast.

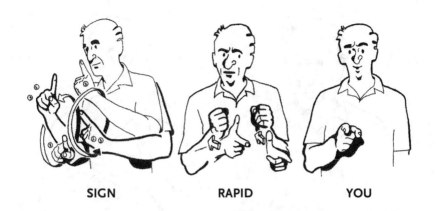

SIGN   RAPID   YOU

I don't understand.

UNDERSTAND

Would you write it, please?

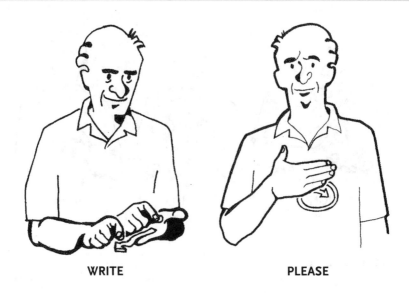

WRITE   PLEASE

How do you sign _____? What's the sign for _____?

Ask these questions by pointing to whatever it is you want to know the sign for or by fingerspelling the word.

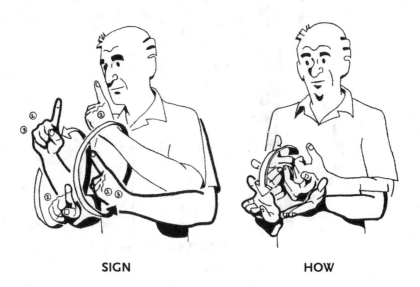

SIGN   HOW

There's no sign for that; you have to fingerspell it.

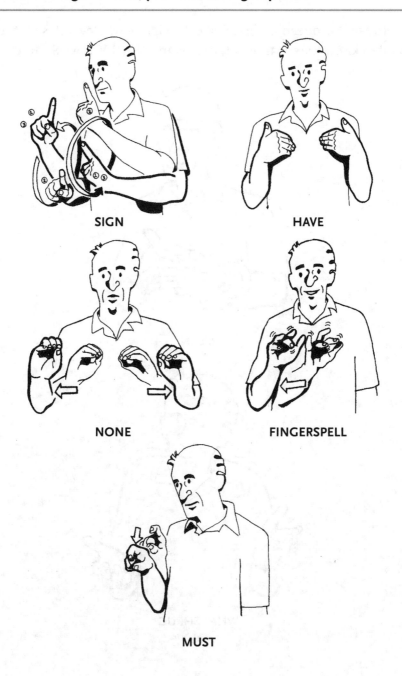

SIGN

HAVE

NONE

FINGERSPELL

MUST

What does _____ mean?

To ask this question, first make the sign of whatever it is that you want to know the meaning of, then sign MEAN WHAT SHRUG.

MEAN

WHAT SHRUG

Are you deaf?

Either way of signing "deaf" is acceptable, but deaf people use the first one shown below more often than the second one.

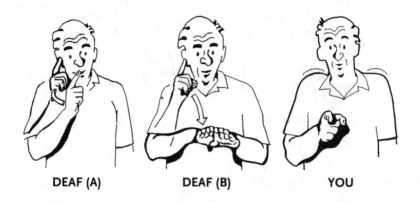

| DEAF (A) | DEAF (B) | YOU |

I'm not deaf, I'm hearing.

Hearing people are referred to as "speaking" people.

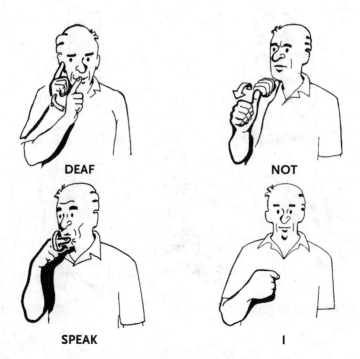

DEAF   NOT

SPEAK   I

I'm hard of hearing.

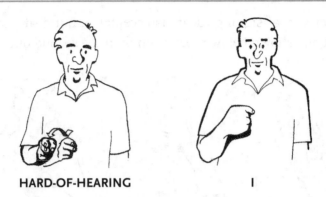

HARD-OF-HEARING   **I**

Do you use a hearing aid?

The first two signs for "hearing aid" shown here represent the kind of aid that is attached by a cord to a unit worn on the body. The third kind is the type worn behind the ear.

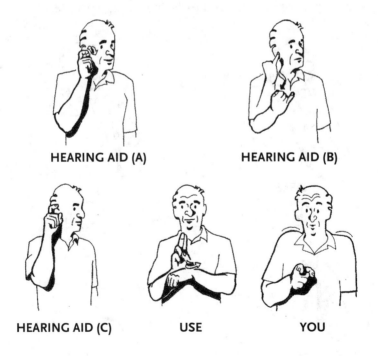

HEARING AID (A)   **HEARING AID (B)**

HEARING AID (C)   **USE**   **YOU**

Can you read lips?

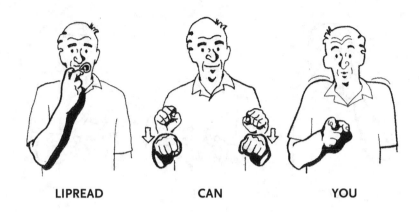

| LIPREAD | CAN | YOU |

I speak a little.

| SPEAK | LITTLE BIT |

How did you lose your hearing?

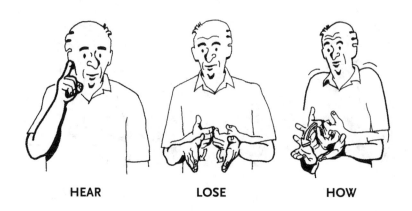

HEAR   LOSE   HOW

How old were you when you became deaf?

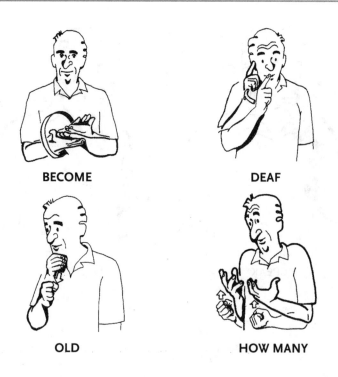

BECOME   DEAF

OLD   HOW MANY

I was born deaf.

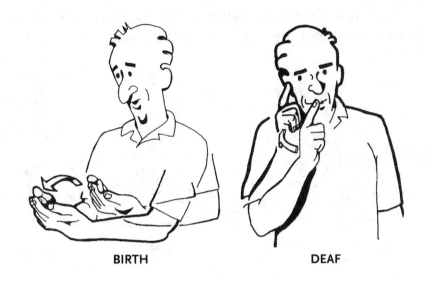

BIRTH   DEAF

Are your parents deaf?

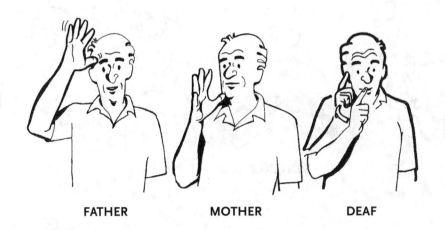

FATHER   MOTHER   DEAF

I want to visit the club for deaf people.

Fingerspell CLUB at the beginning of this sentence. It is not necessary to sign "for deaf people," because the word *club* implies that.

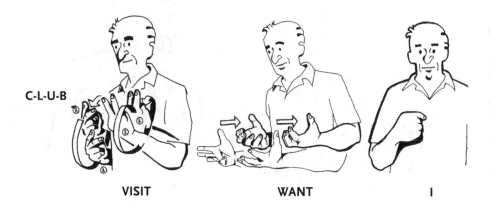

C-L-U-B   VISIT   WANT   I

I enjoy TV with captions.

TV   SENTENCE   PLEASE   I

I saw a captioned film last night.

Note: See Chapter 18 for more phrases on open and closed captioning.

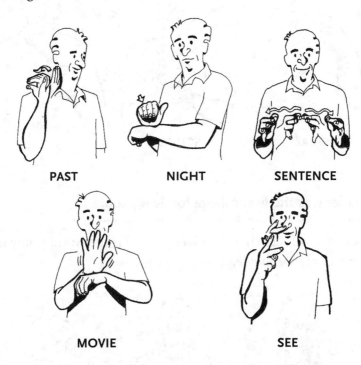

PAST NIGHT SENTENCE

MOVIE SEE

Did you go to a residential school for deaf children?

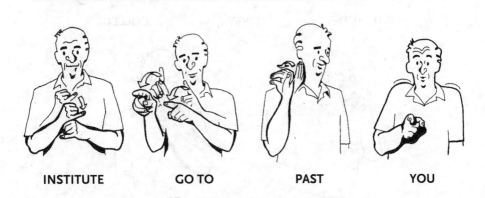

INSTITUTE GO TO PAST YOU

I went to a school for hearing children.

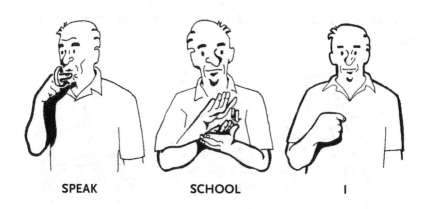

SPEAK   SCHOOL   I

Gallaudet was the first college for deaf people.

Note: Gallaudet is now a university and is the world's only liberal arts university for the deaf.

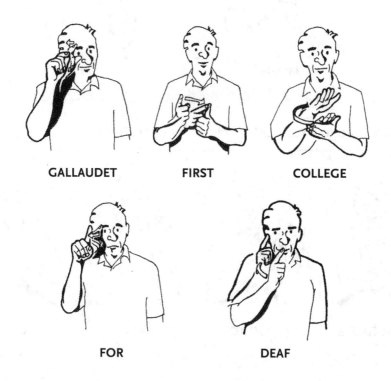

GALLAUDET   FIRST   COLLEGE

FOR   DEAF

Many deaf students enter hearing colleges.

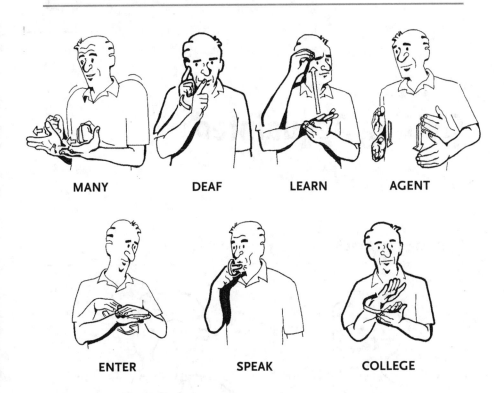

MANY   DEAF   LEARN   AGENT

ENTER   SPEAK   COLLEGE

Gallaudet University is in Washington, D.C.

Sometimes the letters "D-C" are fingerspelled after the sign for "Washington."

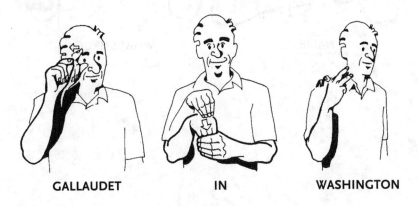

GALLAUDET   IN   WASHINGTON

5

Getting Acquainted

What is your name?

NAME   WHAT SHRUG

My name is _____.

Fingerspell your name.

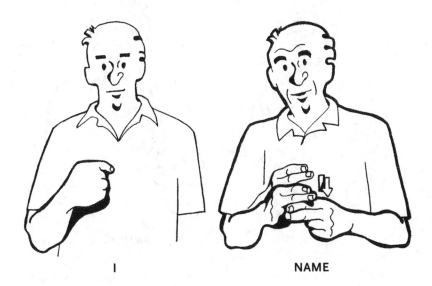

I

NAME

I'm happy to meet you.

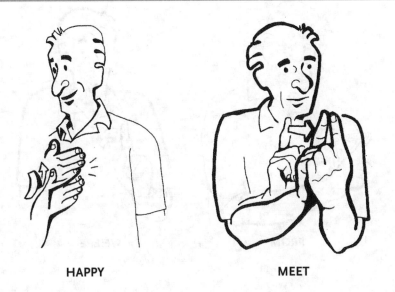

HAPPY

MEET

Where do you live?

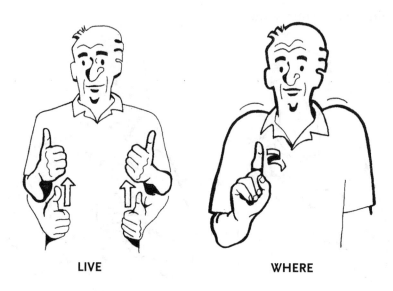

LIVE   WHERE

Where are you from?

FROM   WHERE

Where were you born?

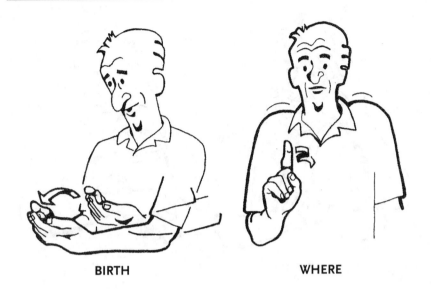

BIRTH WHERE

May I introduce my wife?

After making the sign for the person you are introducing, you then fingerspell that person's name.

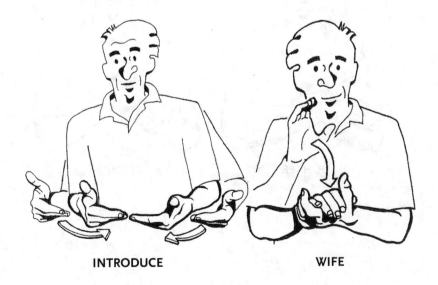

INTRODUCE WIFE

Additional vocabulary

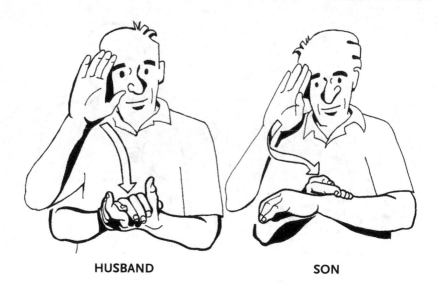

HUSBAND   SON

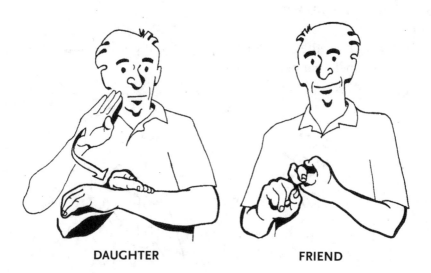

DAUGHTER   FRIEND

Where do you work?

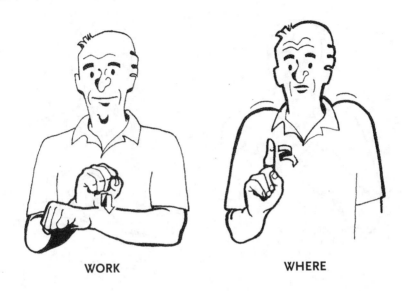

WORK   WHERE

What kind of work do you do?

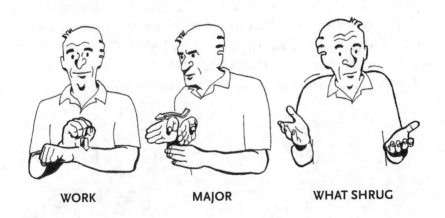

WORK   MAJOR   WHAT SHRUG

I'm a doctor.

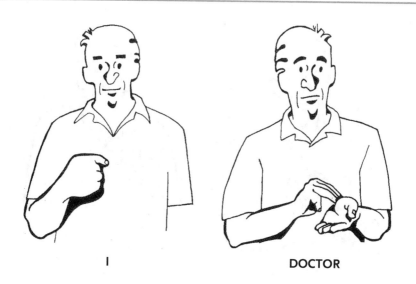

I   DOCTOR

Additional vocabulary

The AGENT sign is often added to a verb or noun sign to indicate that one does or is what the verb or noun sign says. Here the AGENT sign could be added to TEACH, LAW, ACT, and ART, but would not be added to DOCTOR, POLICE, HOMEMAKER, or FIREFIGHTER. The use of the AGENT sign is optional.

LAW   TEACH

ACT

ART

AGENT

FIREFIGHTER

POLICE

Homemaker

Note: To sign "househusband," use the signs for HOUSE and HUSBAND (see page 112). The phrase below cannot be used for a househusband.

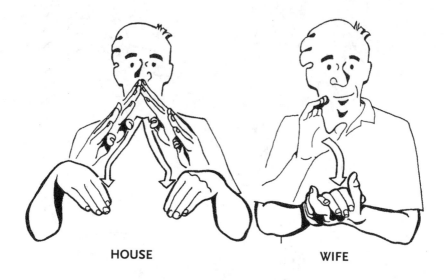

HOUSE   WIFE

Do you go to school?

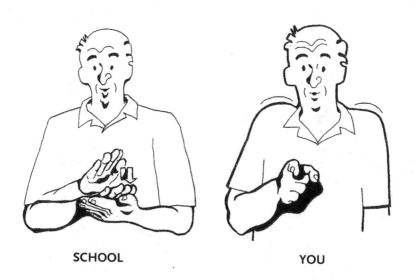

SCHOOL   YOU

Are you married?

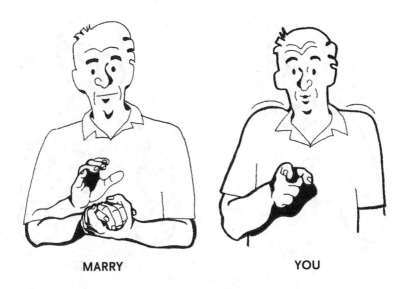

MARRY   YOU

I'm single.

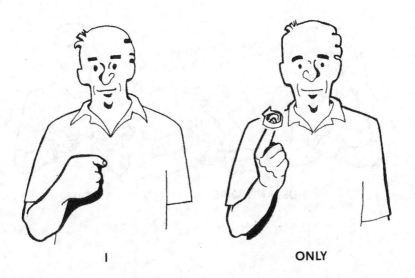

I   ONLY

I'm divorced.

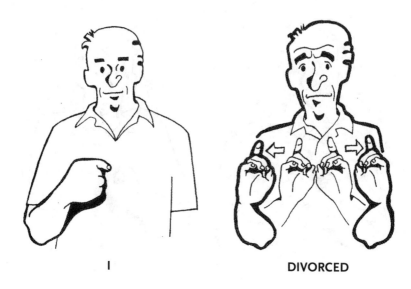

I   DIVORCED

My husband/wife is dead.

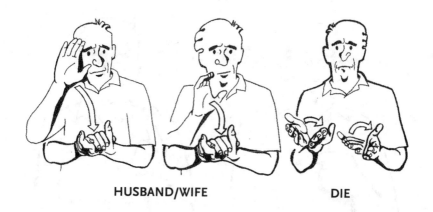

HUSBAND/WIFE   DIE

Do you have any children?

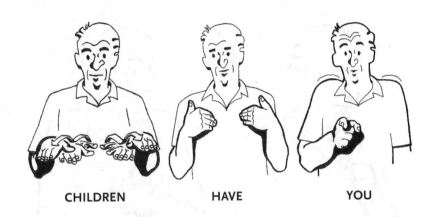

CHILDREN   HAVE   YOU

How many children do you have?

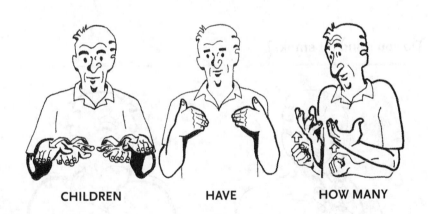

CHILDREN   HAVE   HOW MANY

How old are you?

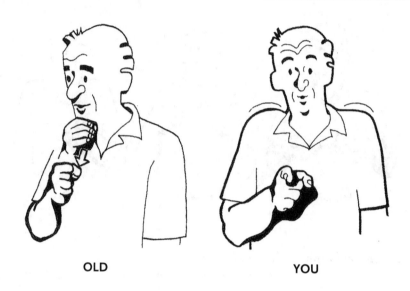

OLD   YOU

Do you mind if I smoke?

SMOKE CIGARETTE   COMPLAIN

It's all right. It's OK.

ALL RIGHT

Smoking is not allowed.

SMOKE CIGARETTE   **PROHIBIT**

6

Health

How do you feel?

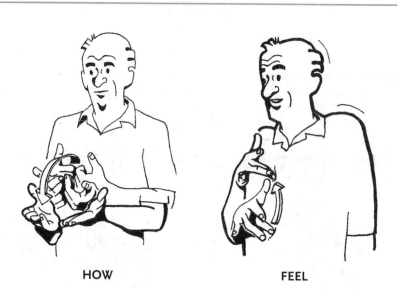

HOW   FEEL

Do you feel all right?

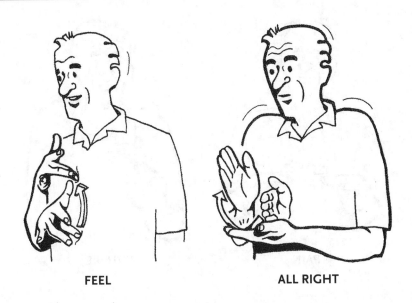

FEEL   ALL RIGHT

I don't feel well.

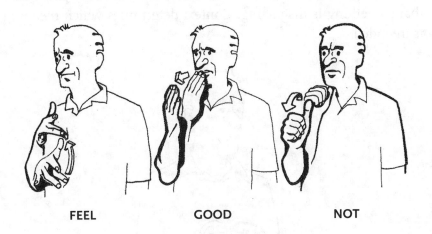

FEEL   GOOD   NOT

Where does it hurt?

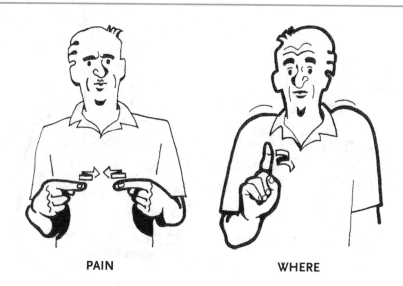

PAIN   WHERE

My stomach is upset.

When done alone, as it is done here, this sign may also mean that something is disgusting. Context determines which meaning is intended.

DISGUST

I have a cold.

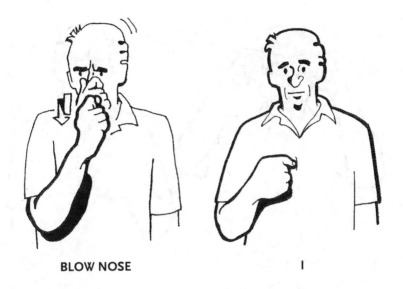

BLOW NOSE   I

My nose is runny.

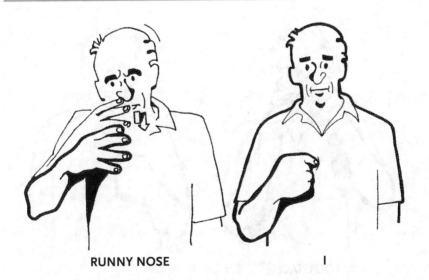

RUNNY NOSE   I

My head aches.

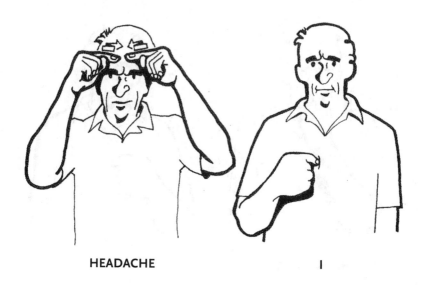

HEADACHE   I

I have a toothache.

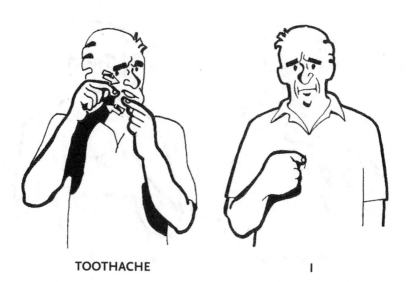

TOOTHACHE   I

I have a stomachache.

The sign PAIN may be placed anywhere on the body to denote that you are hurt or have a pain in that part of the body.

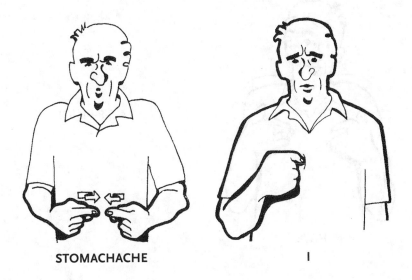

STOMACHACHE   I

I need a dentist/doctor.

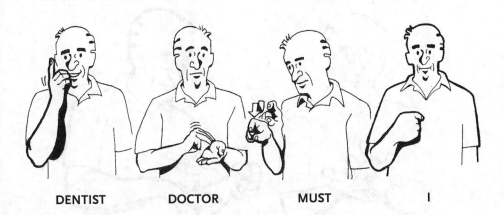

DENTIST   DOCTOR   MUST   I

Do you have any aspirin?

Fingerspell ASPIRIN.

A-S-P-I-R-I-N

HAVE

I've run out of medicine.

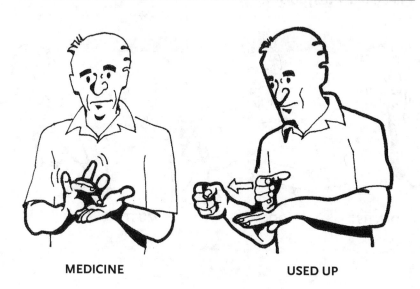

MEDICINE   USED UP

I have to buy some medicine.

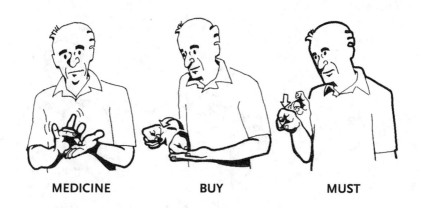

MEDICINE   BUY   MUST

I have to take pills.

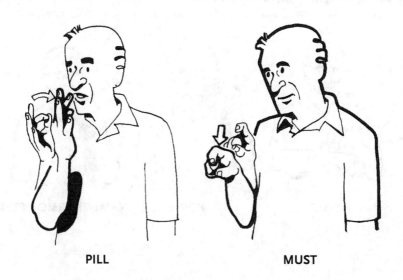

PILL   MUST

You need to have an x-ray.

Fingerspell X-RAY.

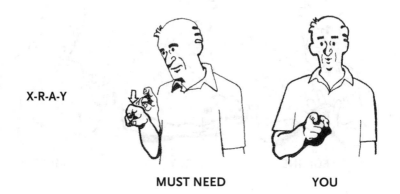

X-R-A-Y   MUST NEED   YOU

It's time to take your temperature.

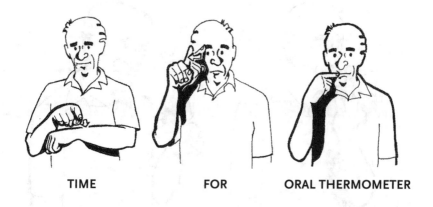

TIME   FOR   ORAL THERMOMETER

You have to have a shot.

The MUST sign may mean "need" or "should" and is done differently depending upon the meaning desired. If something is mandatory, then make one movement down. If something is optional but desirable, then make two gentle downward movements.

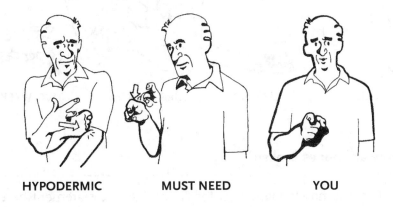

HYPODERMIC   **MUST NEED**   **YOU**

I feel better now.

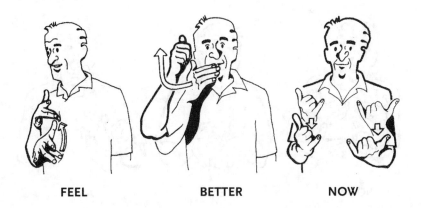

FEEL   **BETTER**   **NOW**

I was in bed for two weeks.

| BED | LIE DOWN | UP TILL NOW | TWO WEEKS |

Were any bones broken?

There is no standard sign for "bone," so the statement here is more generally read as, "Is anything in your body broken?" If you wish to sign "bone" specifically, then you must fingerspell it or find out what the local sign for it is.

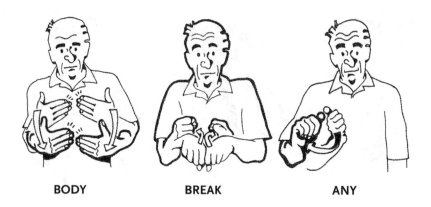

| BODY | BREAK | ANY |

You lost a lot of blood.

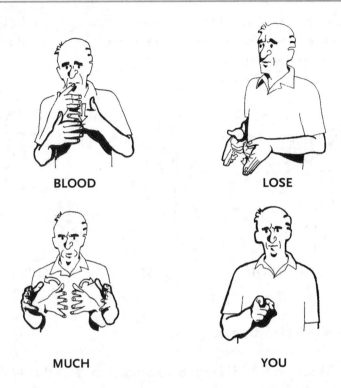

BLOOD

LOSE

MUCH

YOU

They have to draw some blood.

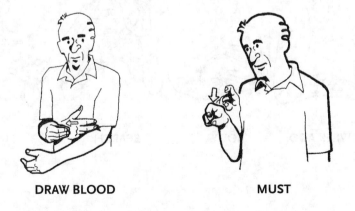

DRAW BLOOD

MUST

Have you ever had a tooth pulled?

The signs PAST and FINISH both refer to the past. Either one may be used alone here, but it is very common to see them both appear in a statement.

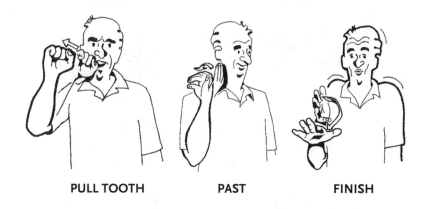

PULL TOOTH   PAST   FINISH

I had a physical last week.

The use of the FINISH sign here denotes the idea that I "already" had a physical last week.

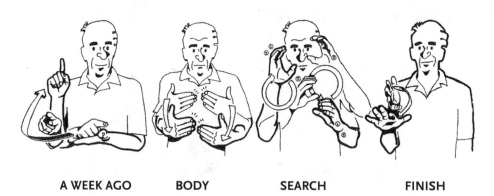

A WEEK AGO   BODY   SEARCH   FINISH

My husband had an operation.

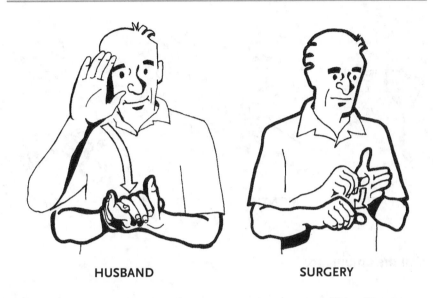

HUSBAND   SURGERY

My wife is in the hospital.

The HOSPITAL sign is made by drawing a cross on the sleeve.

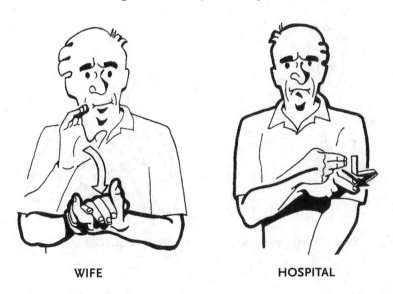

WIFE   HOSPITAL

My father passed away last month.

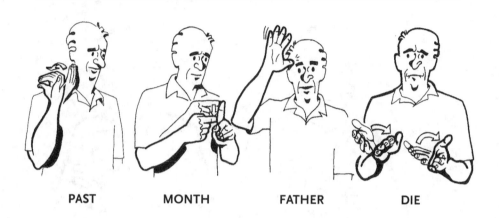

PAST   MONTH   FATHER   DIE

Call the ambulance.

The sign for "ambulance" indicates the spinning red light on top of the vehicle and may refer to any emergency vehicle or just the flashing red light itself. Also, instead of the sign BECKON, you may sign PHONE.

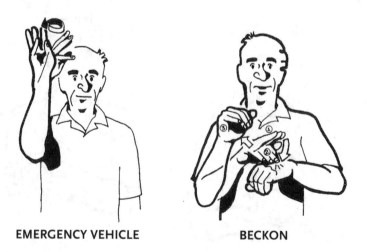

EMERGENCY VEHICLE   BECKON

Do you have hospitalization insurance?

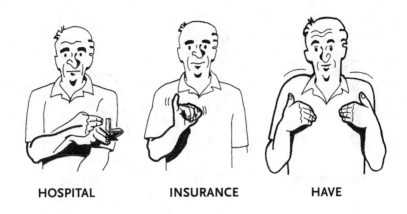

HOSPITAL   INSURANCE   HAVE

I have an appointment at 2:30.

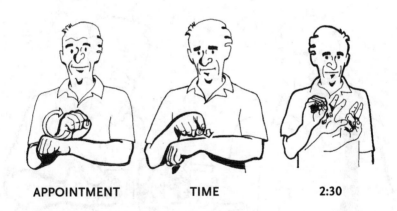

APPOINTMENT   TIME   2:30

Where's my toothbrush?

TOOTHBRUSH   MY   WHERE

I want to brush my teeth.

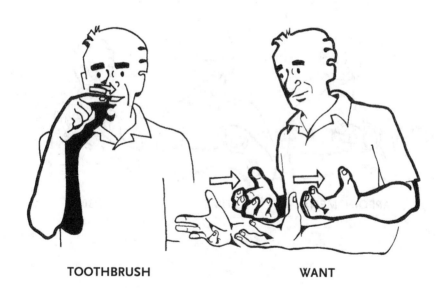

TOOTHBRUSH   WANT

I already took a bath/shower.

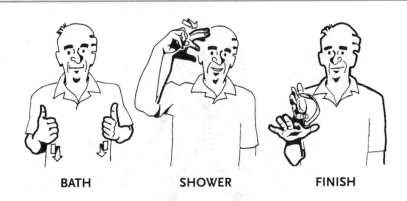

BATH   SHOWER   FINISH

Wash your hands.

This sign, shown in three steps, is a mime of actually washing the hands, as the sign at the top of page 140 is a mime of actually washing the face.

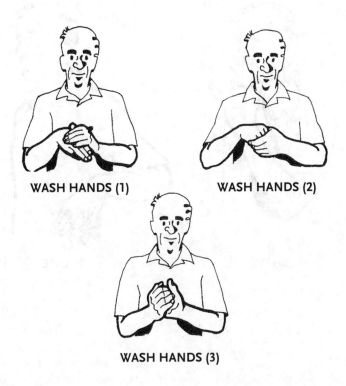

WASH HANDS (1)   WASH HANDS (2)

WASH HANDS (3)

Wash your face.

WASH FACE

I haven't shaved yet.

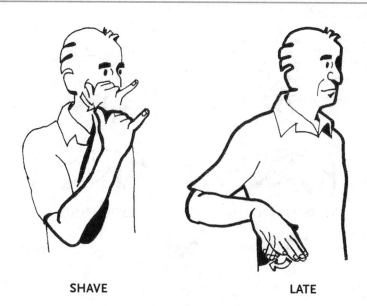

SHAVE   **LATE**

May I borrow your hair dryer?

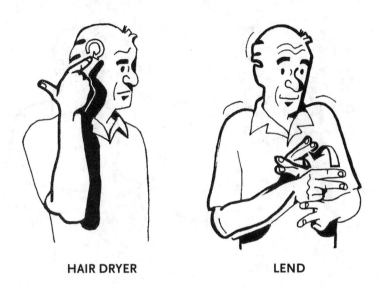

HAIR DRYER

LEND

Brush your hair.

BRUSH HAIR

I lost my comb.

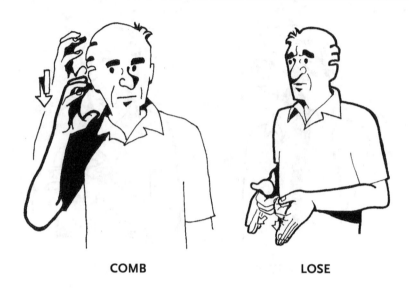

COMB   LOSE

7

Weather

It's beautiful today.

NOW   DAY   PRETTY

The sun is hot.

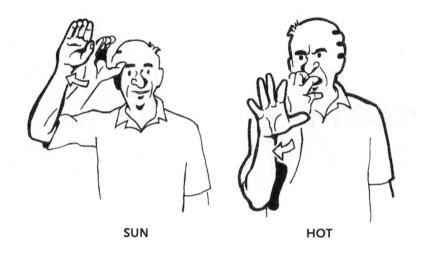

SUN HOT

I enjoy sitting in the sun.

SIT SUNRAY PLEASE

It was cold this morning.

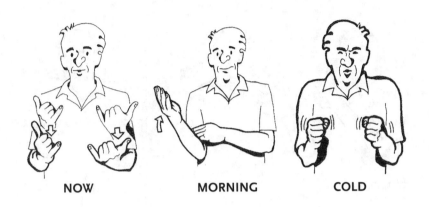

NOW   MORNING   COLD

It will freeze tonight.

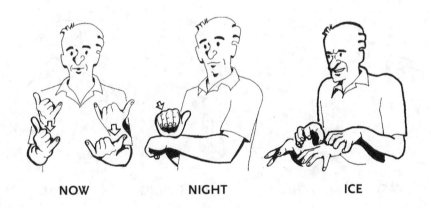

NOW   NIGHT   ICE

Maybe it will snow tomorrow.

TOMORROW   SNOW   MAYBE

There was thunder and lightning last night.

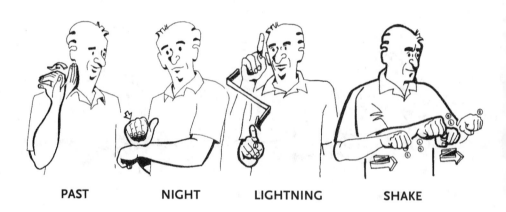

PAST   NIGHT   LIGHTNING   SHAKE

It rained yesterday.

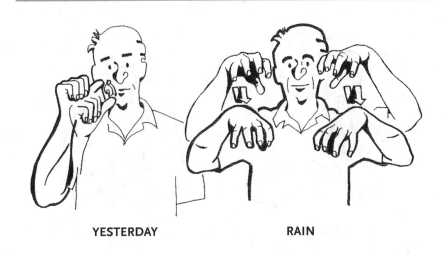

YESTERDAY   RAIN

Do you have a raincoat?

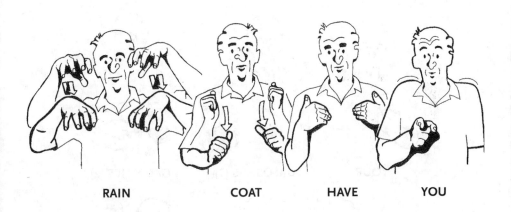

RAIN COAT HAVE YOU

I lost my umbrella.

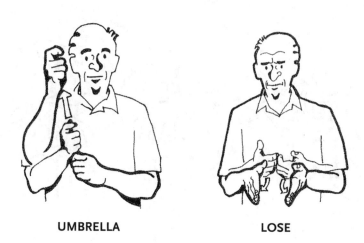

UMBRELLA

LOSE

Where are your galoshes/rubbers?

YOUR

GALOSHES (1)

GALOSHES (2)

RUBBER

WHERE

It's windy today.

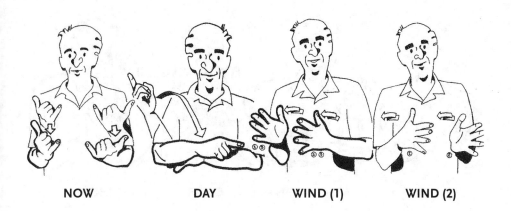

| NOW | DAY | WIND (1) | WIND (2) |

Yesterday evening at sunset, the clouds were beautiful.

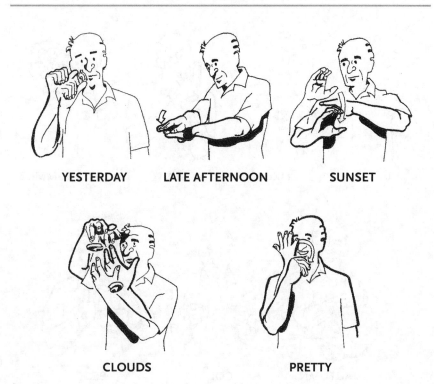

| YESTERDAY | LATE AFTERNOON | SUNSET |

| CLOUDS | PRETTY |

I hope it clears up this afternoon.

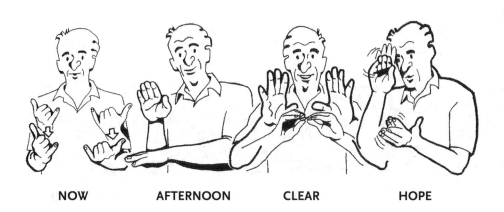

NOW   AFTERNOON   CLEAR   HOPE

I like spring/summer/autumn/winter best.

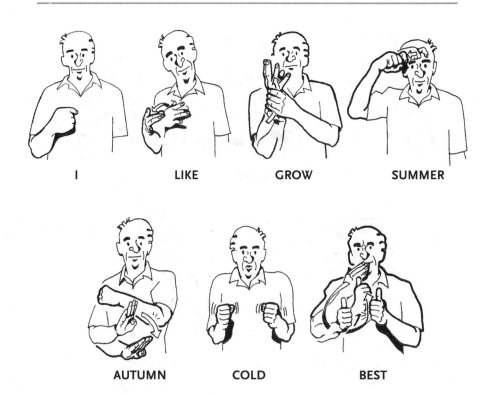

I   LIKE   GROW   SUMMER

AUTUMN   COLD   BEST

You have to have chains to drive in the mountains in winter.

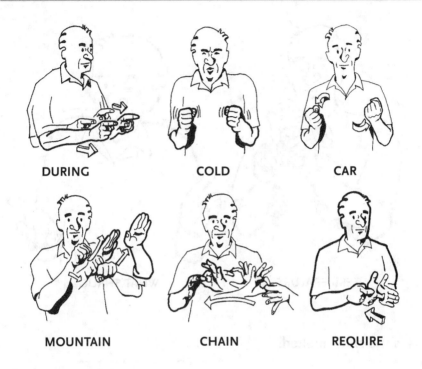

DURING   COLD   CAR

MOUNTAIN   CHAIN   REQUIRE

I'm afraid of tornados.

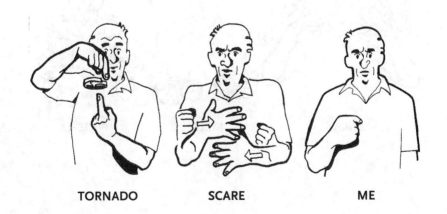

TORNADO   SCARE   ME

What's the temperature?

TEMPERATURE   WHAT SHRUG

Has the snow melted?

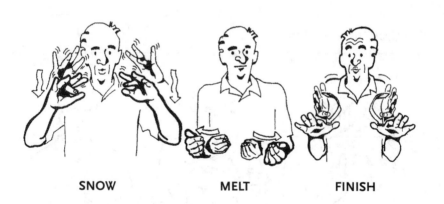

SNOW   MELT   FINISH

There was a flood last year.

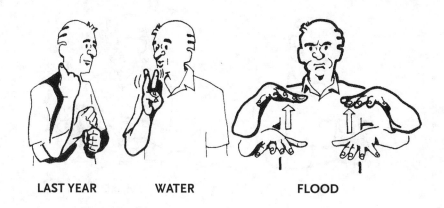

LAST YEAR   WATER   FLOOD

The temperature is below zero.

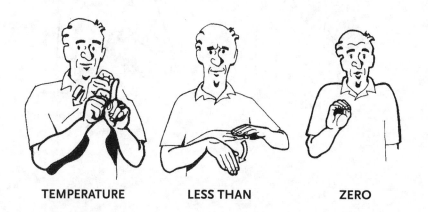

TEMPERATURE   LESS THAN   ZERO

Have you ever been in an earthquake?

EARTH   SHAKE

FINISH   YOU

8

Family

Your father is nice looking.

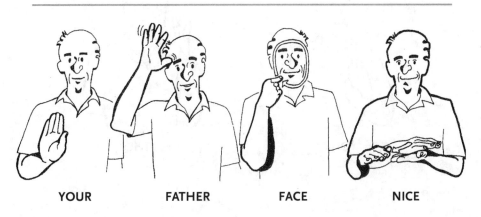

| YOUR | FATHER | FACE | NICE |

You look like your mother.

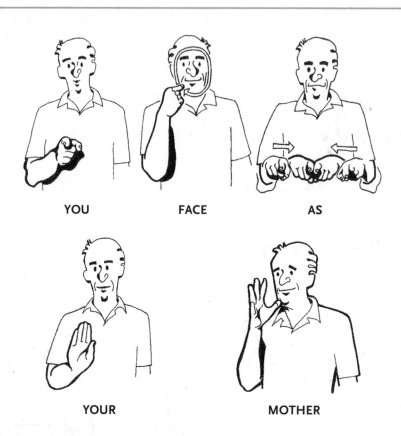

YOU   FACE   AS

YOUR   MOTHER

My brother is younger than I.

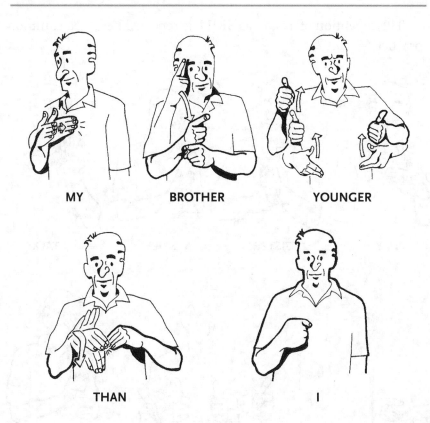

MY   BROTHER   YOUNGER

THAN   I

My sister speaks several languages fluently.

The repetition of a sign, as SKILL is repeated here, is a common practice.

MY   SISTER   SKILL   TALK

FEW   LANGUAGE   SKILL

His son wants to be an astronaut.

HIS/HER/ITS SON AIM

ROCKET AGENT

Her daughter works here.

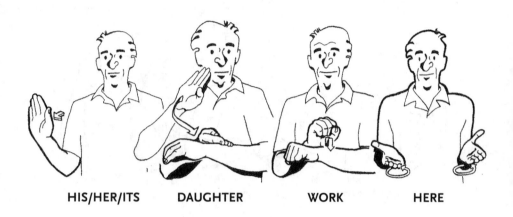

HIS/HER/ITS   DAUGHTER   WORK   HERE

My uncle is a farmer.

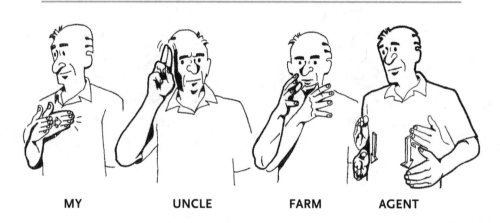

MY   UNCLE   FARM   AGENT

My aunt lives in town.

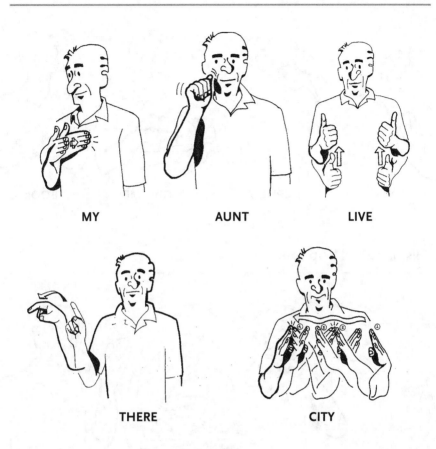

MY   AUNT   LIVE

THERE   CITY

Your nephew gave me a book.

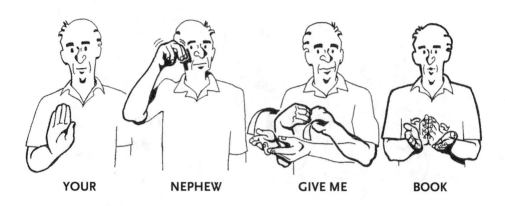

YOUR   NEPHEW   GIVE ME   BOOK

His niece will help you.

HIS/HER/ITS   NIECE   SHE HELP YOU   WILL

Her grandfather gave her grandmother a book.

Normally the sign GRANDMOTHER would have been made with the right hand, but since the action of the GIVE sign moves from the signer's right to the signer's left, making the GRANDMOTHER sign with the left hand makes it visually clearer who is on which side. (For further explanation, see the "Placement of Signs" section in Chapter 2.)

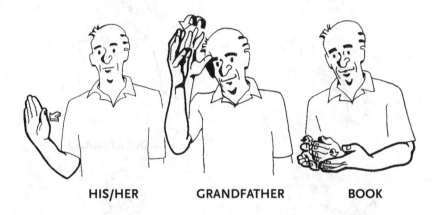

HIS/HER   GRANDFATHER   BOOK

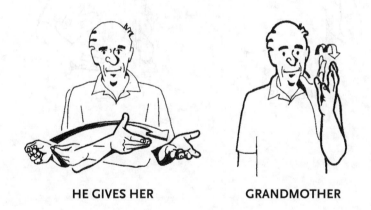

HE GIVES HER   GRANDMOTHER

My cousin is a pilot.

Note: American Sign Language distinguishes between male and female cousins: the signs are gender-specific. Here, the sign is for a male cousin. For a female cousin, use the same sign handshape but in a different location: the jaw area.

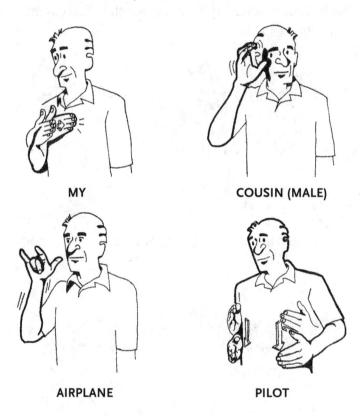

MY **COUSIN (MALE)**

AIRPLANE **PILOT**

Who is that man?

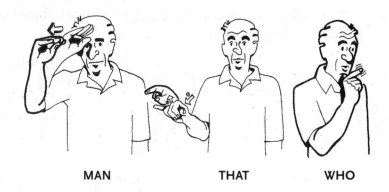

MAN   THAT   WHO

Did you see the woman?

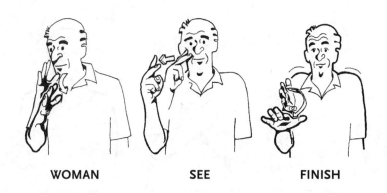

WOMAN   SEE   FINISH

The baby is cute.

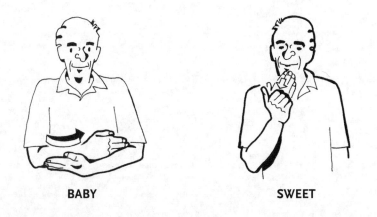

BABY   SWEET

The girl told the boy that she loves him.

The use of both hands in making the sign helps reinforce visually who is doing what to whom.

GIRL   HE/SHE/IT   TELL   BOY

HE/SHE/IT   LOVE   HIM/HER/IT

Father told the little boy to play outside.

The TELL sign moves downward to denote that the person being told is a child. The same thing occurs in the following sentence with the HER sign.

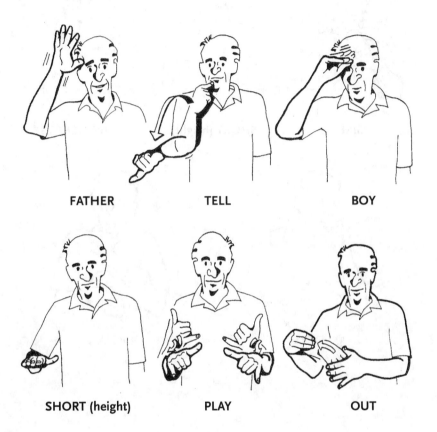

FATHER   TELL   BOY

SHORT (height)   PLAY   OUT

The little girl's doll is broken.

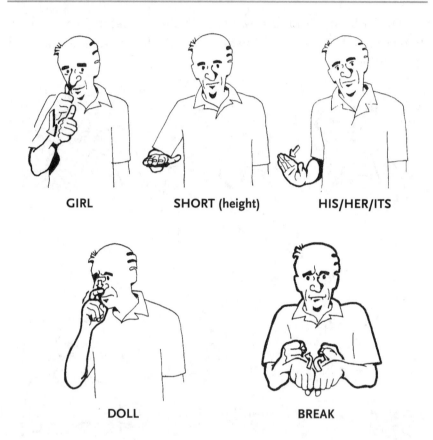

GIRL   SHORT (height)   HIS/HER/ITS

DOLL   BREAK

How many children are coming?

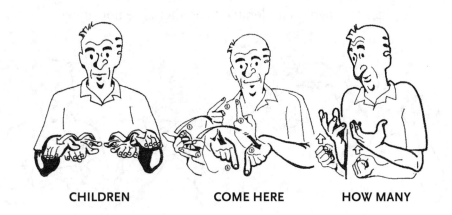

CHILDREN   COME HERE   HOW MANY

Our family is large/small.

OUR   FAMILY   LARGE   SMALL

We had a family reunion last summer.

The idea "we had" is understood and therefore not signed.

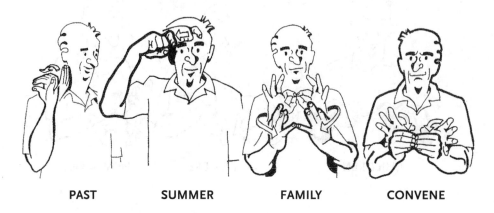

PAST   SUMMER   FAMILY   CONVENE

We met at Grandfather's farm.

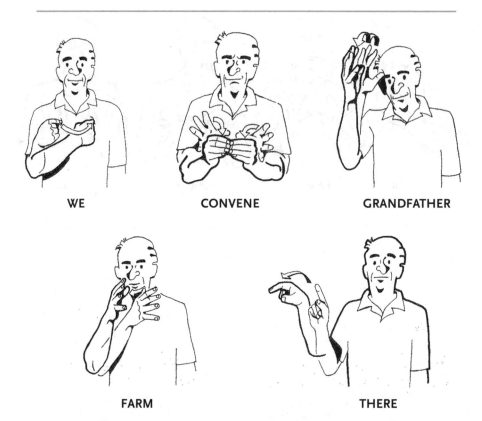

WE   CONVENE   GRANDFATHER

FARM   THERE

Additional vocabulary

ADOPT (+ daughter/son/brother/sister)

FOSTER (+ children/daughter/son/brother/sister)*

STEP (+ father/mother/brother/sister)

*The same sign is used for FOSTER and FALSE; the context of the sentence will determine which concept is being conveyed.

HALF (+ brother/sister)

IN-LAW
(+ mother/father/daughter/son)

GAY

LESBIAN

PARTNER (A)

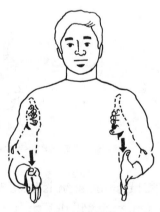

PARTNER (B)

9

School

Do you go to school? Are you in school?

SCHOOL   YOU

I go to college.

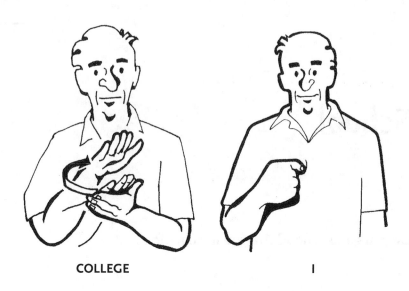

COLLEGE   I

I'm majoring in English.

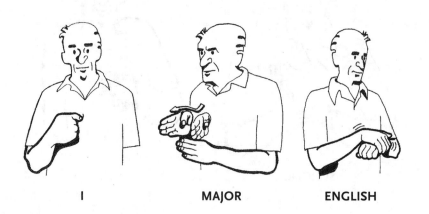

I   MAJOR   ENGLISH

Additional vocabulary for majors or courses of study

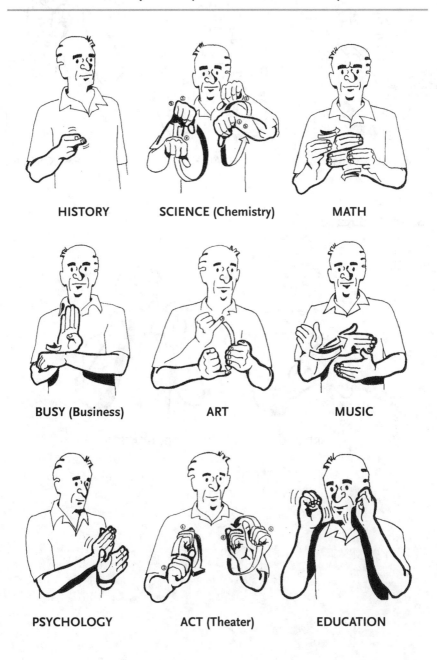

HISTORY   SCIENCE (Chemistry)   MATH

BUSY (Business)   ART   MUSIC

PSYCHOLOGY   ACT (Theater)   EDUCATION

ADVISE (Counseling)

HEALTH

PHILOSOPHY

Special education

SPECIAL

EDUCATION

Physical therapy

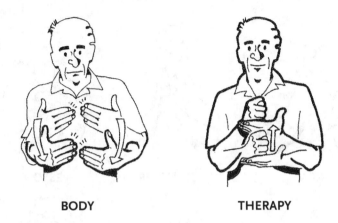

BODY   THERAPY

Computer science

The sign for "computer" varies a good deal around the country, so check it out with your local deaf people. See also Chapter 18, "Technology."

COMPUTER

Other academic fields are fingerspelled, either in full or in abbreviated form. "Physical Education" is "P-E," "Library Science" is "L-S," "Sociology" is "S-O-C," and so on.

What course are you taking this semester?

NOW   SEMESTER   LESSON

LESSON (rear view)   TAKE UP   WHAT SHRUG

I'm a student.

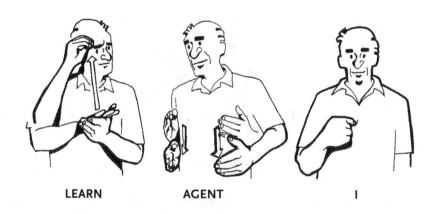

LEARN   AGENT   I

Additional vocabulary

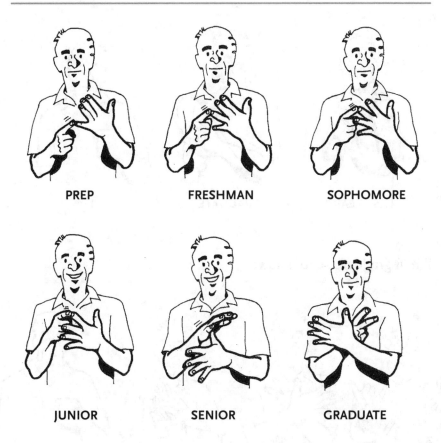

PREP   FRESHMAN   SOPHOMORE

JUNIOR   SENIOR   GRADUATE

I graduated last year.

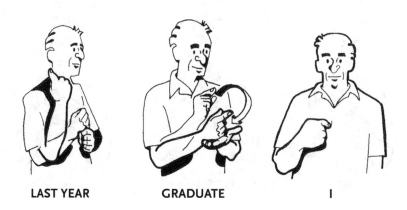

LAST YEAR   GRADUATE   I

I'm in graduate school now.

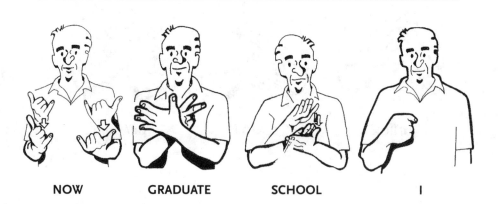

NOW   GRADUATE   SCHOOL   I

I like to study.

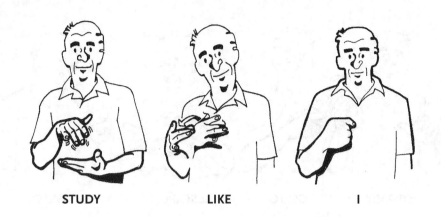

STUDY   LIKE   I

Where's the administration building?

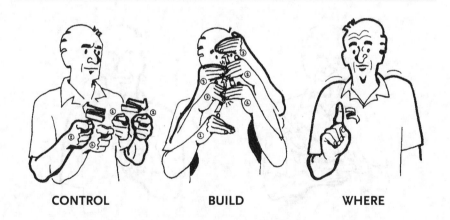

CONTROL   BUILD   WHERE

You've got to go to the library and do some research.

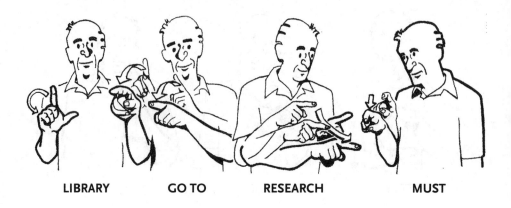

LIBRARY   GO TO   RESEARCH   MUST

I got an A on my paper.

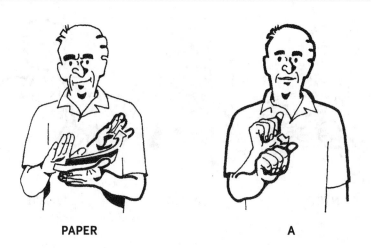

PAPER   A

I studied all night.

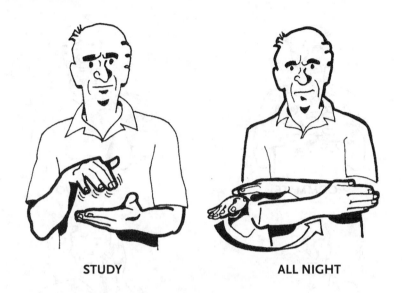

STUDY   ALL NIGHT

Where's my calculator?

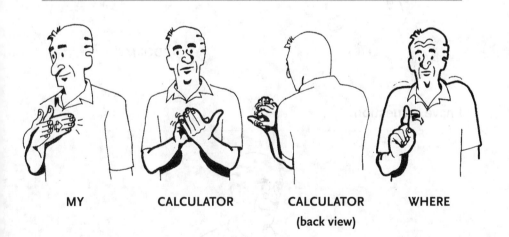

MY   CALCULATOR   CALCULATOR   WHERE
                                (back view)

My roommate and I live in a dorm.

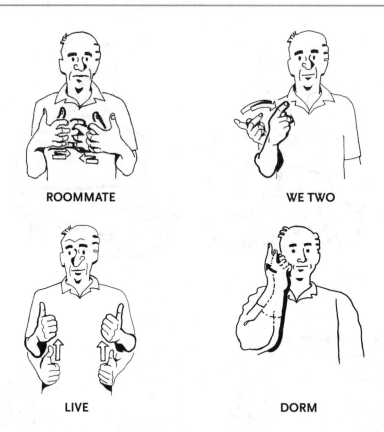

ROOMMATE

WE TWO

LIVE

DORM

I have a question.

QUERY

Did you ask him?

QUERY   FINISH   YOU

The teacher asked me a lot of questions.

The repetition of the QUERY sign using both hands indicates that many questions were asked.

TEACH   QUERY ME

No talking during the test.

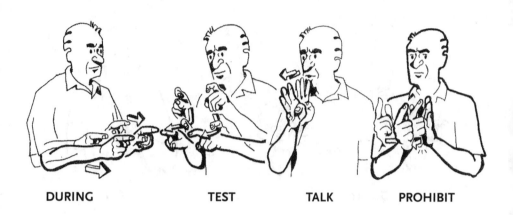

DURING   TEST   TALK   PROHIBIT

We have a test tomorrow.

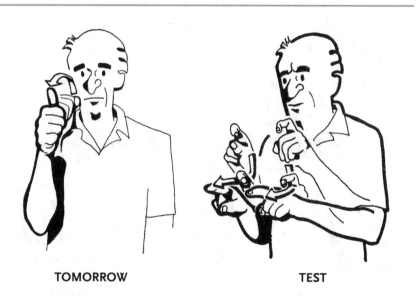

TOMORROW   TEST

Close your books.

CLOSE BOOK

Open your books.

OPEN BOOK

Begin writing.

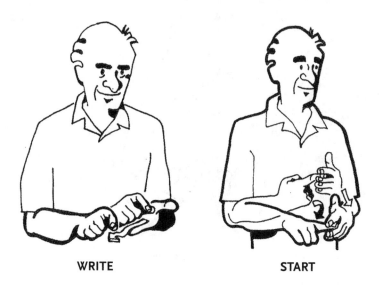

WRITE   START

Stop writing.

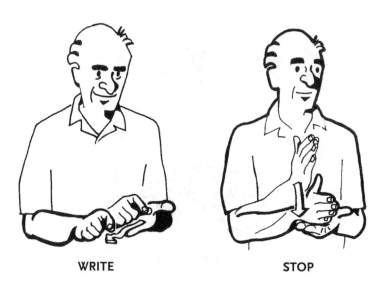

WRITE   STOP

I lost my pencil.

The sign WRITE also stands for "pen," "pencil," and any other writing instrument.

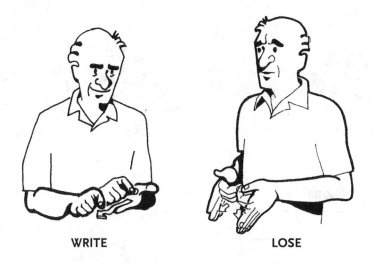

WRITE LOSE

Please don't erase the board.

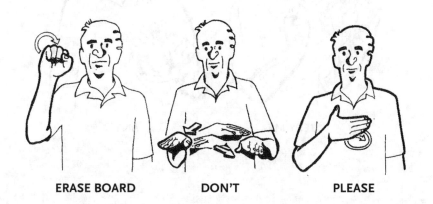

ERASE BOARD DON'T PLEASE

Did you pass or fail/flunk?

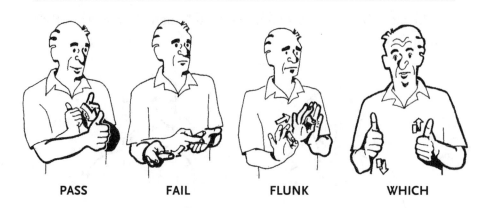

PASS   FAIL   FLUNK   WHICH

Any questions?

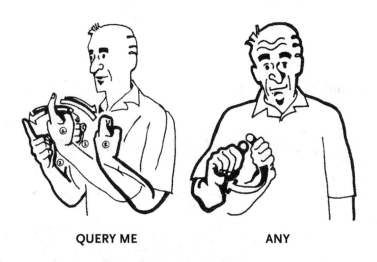

QUERY ME   ANY

You haven't turned in your paper to me yet.

In order to sign GIVE, reverse the movement of the GIVE ME sign.

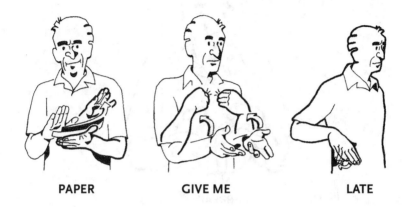

PAPER GIVE ME LATE

She and I discussed it.

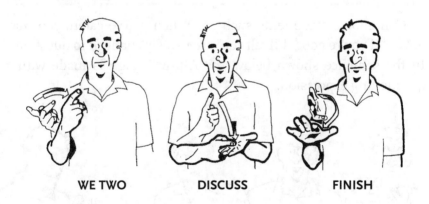

WE TWO DISCUSS FINISH

Let's take a break.

BREAK

When you've been absent, you must bring an excuse.

Conditional statements such as "When you've eaten, you may go" or "If you're good, I'll tell you" are usually changed to questions. In the sentence shown below, the ABSENT sign is made with a questioning expression.

ABSENT   **EXCUSE**   **BRING**   **MUST**

10

Food and Drink

Have you eaten? Did you eat? Are you finished eating?

EAT   FINISH

I haven't eaten yet.

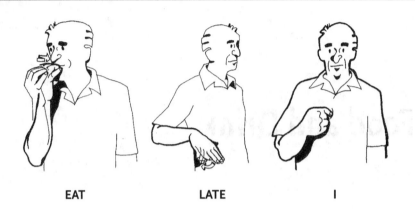

EAT   LATE   I

He eats too much.

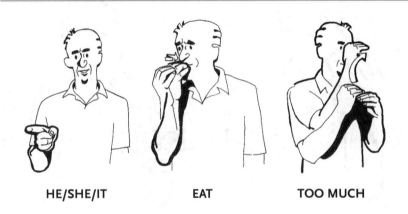

HE/SHE/IT   EAT   TOO MUCH

Are you hungry?

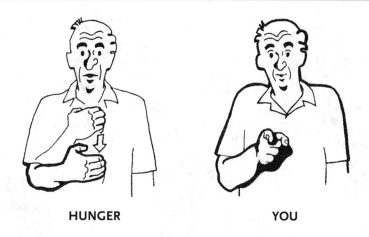

HUNGER   YOU

Let's you and I go to a restaurant.

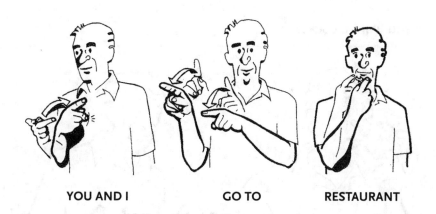

YOU AND I   GO TO   RESTAURANT

What are you going to order?

ORDER   WHAT SHRUG

Do you want a cocktail?

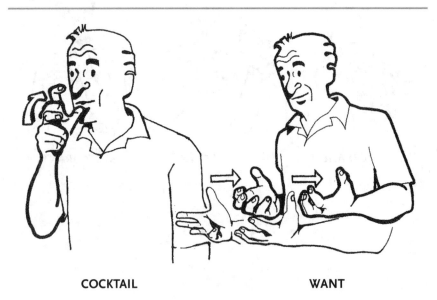

COCKTAIL   WANT

Do you want red or white wine?

RED

WHITE

WINE

WANT

WHICH

I'll have a scotch and water.

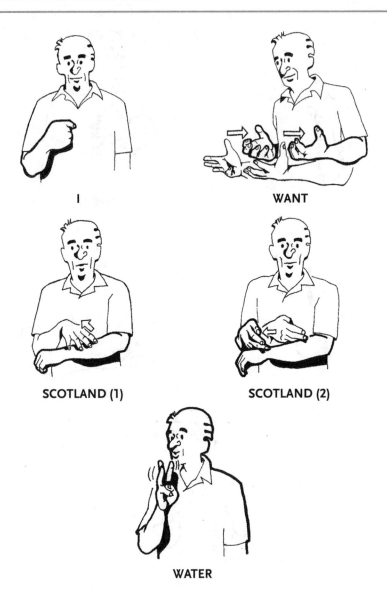

I

WANT

SCOTLAND (1)

SCOTLAND (2)

WATER

They have a lot of different beers.

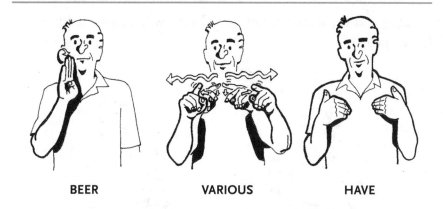

BEER VARIOUS HAVE

He never drinks whiskey.

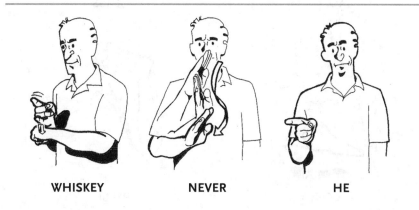

WHISKEY NEVER HE

Do you want a soft drink?

SOFT DRINK (1) SOFT DRINK (2) WANT

I want a tall Coke/Pepsi.

Coke and Pepsi are the only soft drinks with signs; all others are fingerspelled.

TALL (glass)   GLASS

COKE   PEPSI

WANT

I like sandwiches and hamburgers.

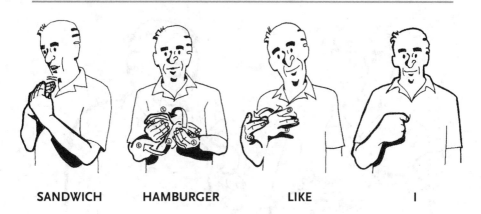

SANDWICH   HAMBURGER   LIKE   I

Where's the waiter/waitress?

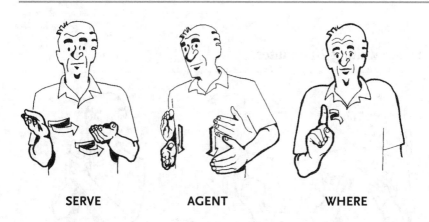

SERVE   AGENT   WHERE

The service is lousy.

SERVE   LOUSY

I've been waiting 20 minutes.

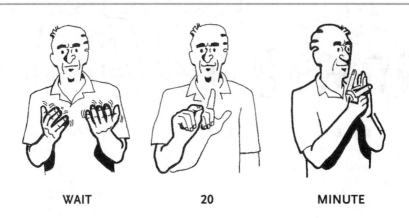

WAIT   20   MINUTE

I want a large/medium/small milk.

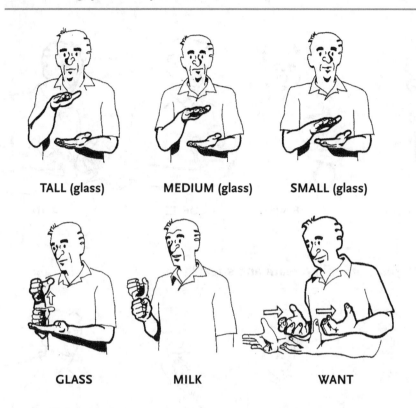

TALL (glass)   MEDIUM (glass)   SMALL (glass)

GLASS   MILK   WANT

I'll have iced/hot tea.

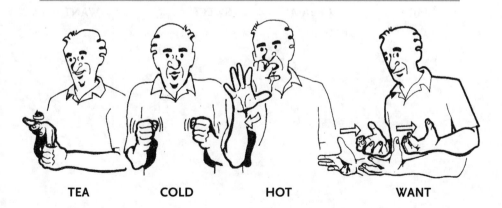

TEA   COLD   HOT   WANT

I'll have coffee after I eat.

EAT   FINISH   COFFEE   WANT

Do you want milk/cream and sugar?

MILK   CREAM   SWEET   WANT

I take it black, please.

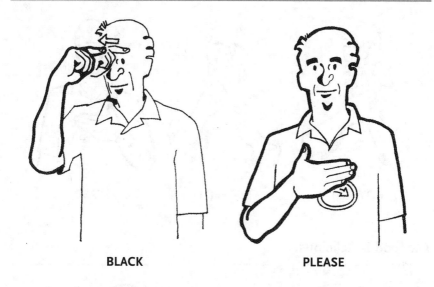

BLACK PLEASE

Sugar only, please.

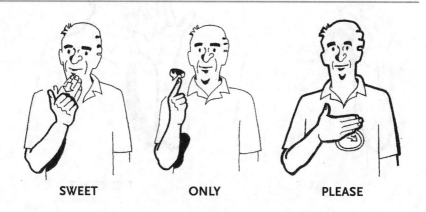

SWEET ONLY PLEASE

Both, please.

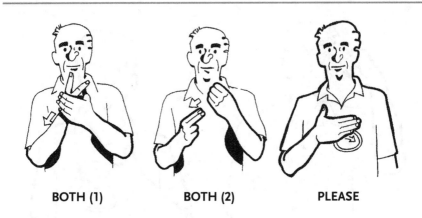

BOTH (1)   BOTH (2)   PLEASE

The food is delicious.

EAT   DELICIOUS

The meat is too rare.

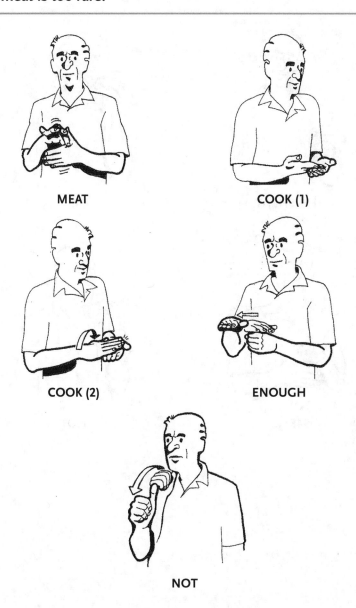

MEAT

COOK (1)

COOK (2)

ENOUGH

NOT

He/she does not eat meat. He/she's a vegetarian.

HE/SHE/IT

EAT

MEAT

NOT

The vegetables are overdone.

V-E-G

COOK (1)

COOK (2)

TOO MUCH

Fingerspell "V-E-G" at the beginning of the sentence. Most vegetables, fruits, and meats are fingerspelled. Some of those that have signs follow.

Additional vocabulary

APPLE   BACON   BANANA

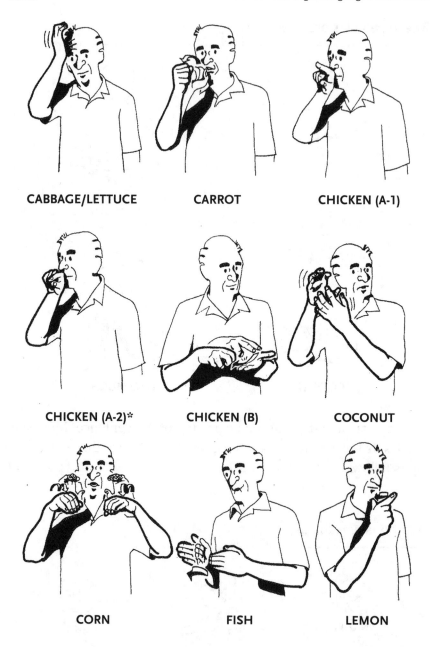

CABBAGE/LETTUCE   CARROT   CHICKEN (A-1)

CHICKEN (A-2)*   CHICKEN (B)   COCONUT

CORN   FISH   LEMON

*This is the sign for "BIRD," but it is often used for "chicken."

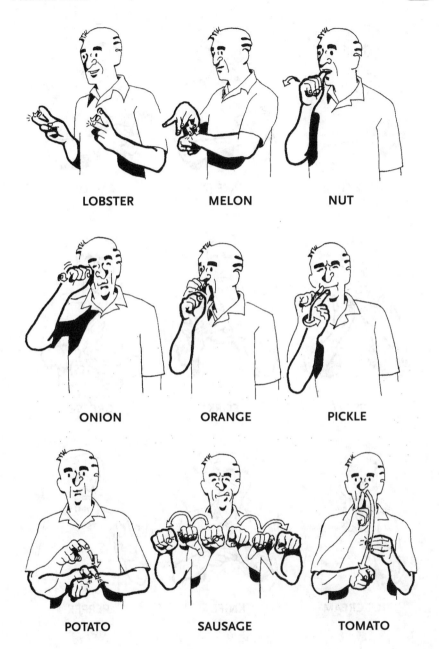

LOBSTER   MELON   NUT

ONION   ORANGE   PICKLE

POTATO   SAUSAGE   TOMATO

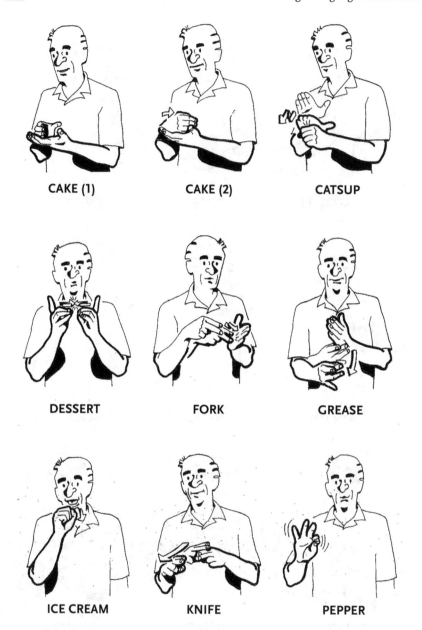

CAKE (1) CAKE (2) CATSUP

DESSERT FORK GREASE

ICE CREAM KNIFE PEPPER

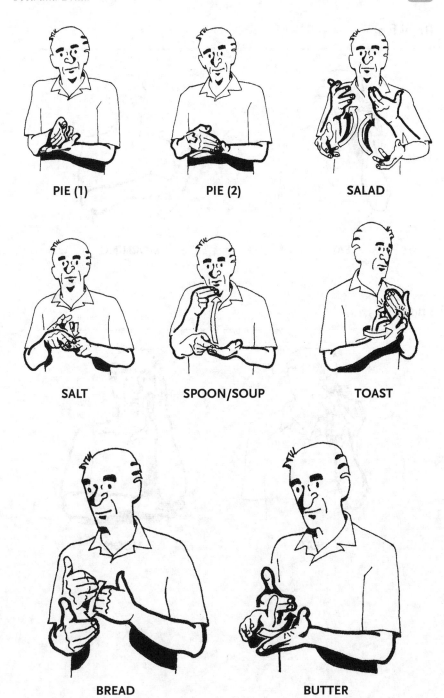

PIE (1)

PIE (2)

SALAD

SALT

SPOON/SOUP

TOAST

BREAD

BUTTER

Breakfast

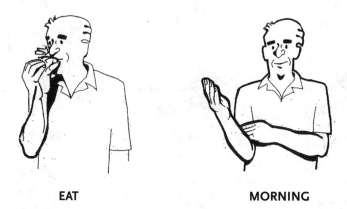

EAT   MORNING

Lunch

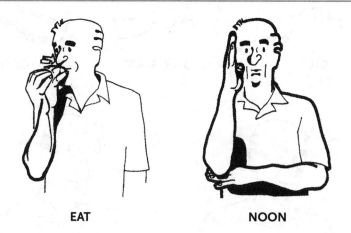

EAT   NOON

Supper/dinner

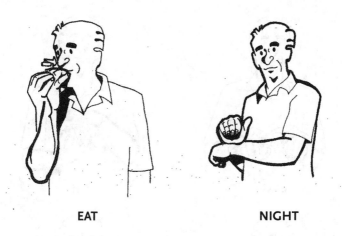

EAT　　　　　　　　NIGHT

The following signs are for describing how you want your eggs.

Scrambled

To indicate whether you want your scrambled eggs moist or dry, sign WET or DRY after EGG MIX.

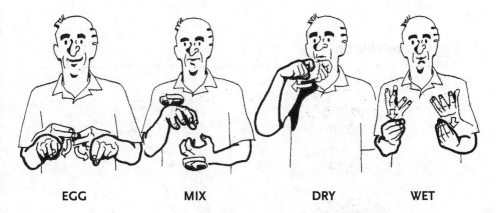

EGG　　　　MIX　　　　DRY　　　　WET

Soft-/hard-boiled eggs

EGG   BOIL

SOFT   HARD

Eggs sunny-side up

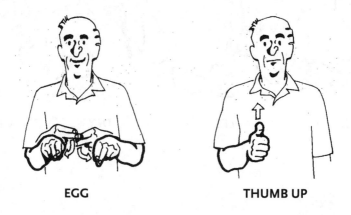

EGG   THUMB UP

Eggs over easy

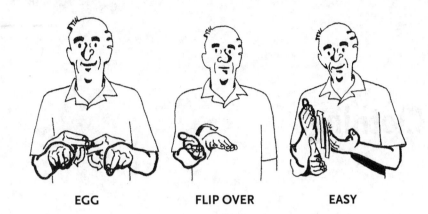

EGG   FLIP OVER   EASY

11

Clothing

I have to go shopping.

The BUY sign is repeated to convey the idea "shopping."

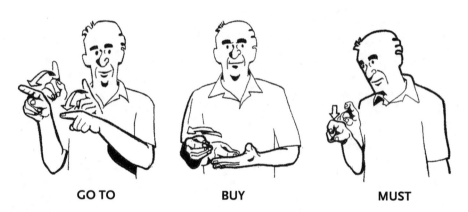

GO TO   BUY   MUST

What are you wearing tonight?

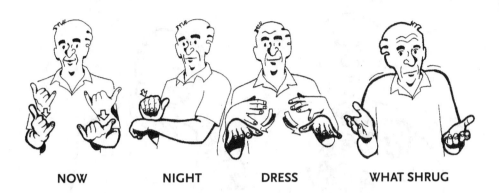

NOW   NIGHT   DRESS   WHAT SHRUG

That dress is an odd color.

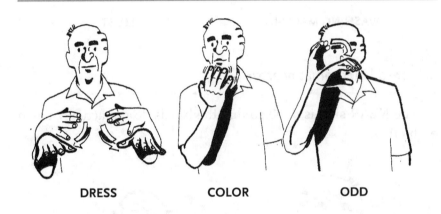

DRESS   COLOR   ODD

Do you have any dirty clothes?

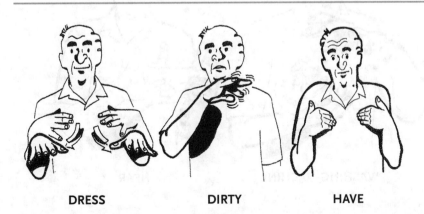

DRESS   DIRTY   HAVE

I need to do some laundry.

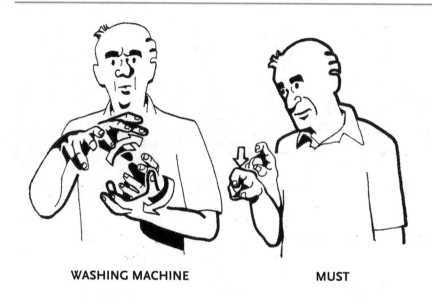

WASHING MACHINE   MUST

Is there a laundromat nearby?

The NEAR sign is done so that the hands do not actually touch each other.

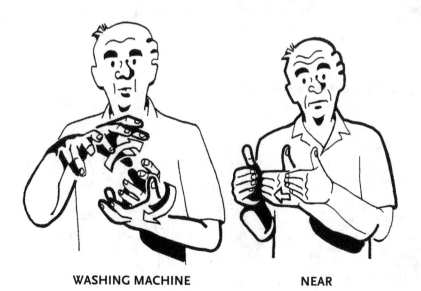

WASHING MACHINE   NEAR

He always dresses nicely.

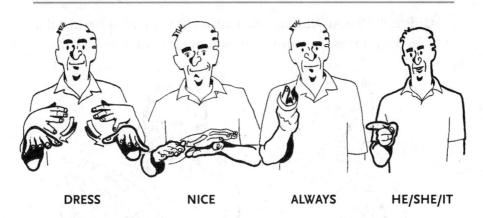

DRESS NICE ALWAYS HE/SHE/IT

The shirt and tie don't match.

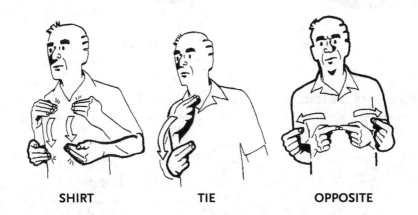

SHIRT TIE OPPOSITE

Blue agrees with you.

Ordinarily the AGREE sign just moves downward, but when it is used in the expression above, it must move toward the watcher.

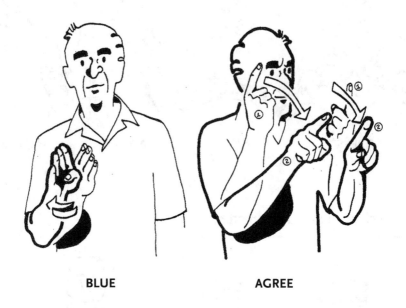

BLUE   AGREE

My trousers are torn.

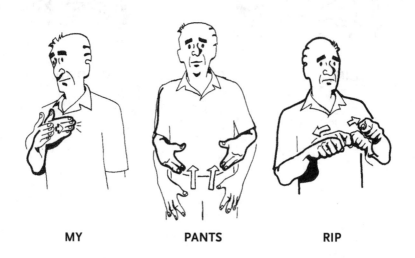

MY   PANTS   RIP

Can you sew a button for me?

Fingerspell BUTTON at the beginning of the sentence before the sign SEW.

B-U-T-T-O-N

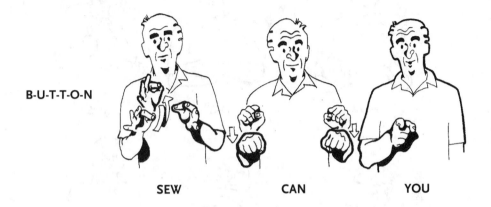

SEW   CAN   YOU

I can't tie a bow tie.

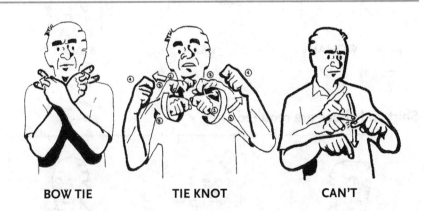

BOW TIE   TIE KNOT   CAN'T

Most women wear slacks nowadays.

NOW   DAY   MOST

WOMAN   USE   SLACKS

Shirt and shoes are required.

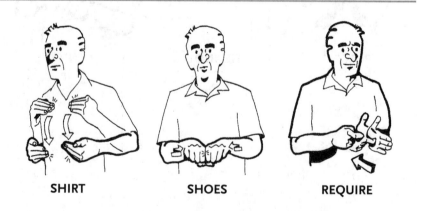

SHIRT   SHOES   REQUIRE

I wear shorts every day in the summer.

DURING	SUMMER	SHORTS

EVERY DAY	I

She needs to wash out her skirt.

SKIRT	WASH CLOTHES	MUST	HE/SHE/IT

Your socks don't match.

SOCKS　　　　SAME　　　　NOT

Who took my hat?

MY　　　　HAT　　　　GRAB　　　　WHO

I can't fasten my belt.

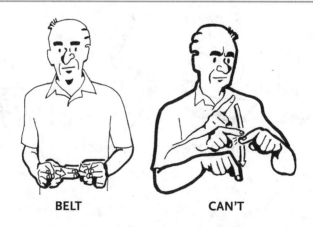

BELT　　　　CAN'T

When I took my coat to the cleaners, it shrunk.

COAT

PUT

CLEANERS

FINISH

SHORTER SLEEVE

12

Sports and Recreation

Do you like to play baseball?

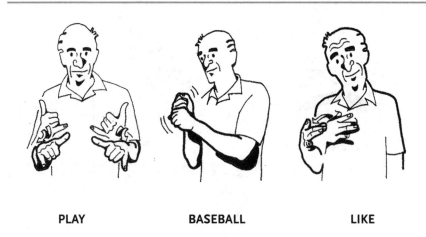

PLAY   BASEBALL   LIKE

Additional vocabulary

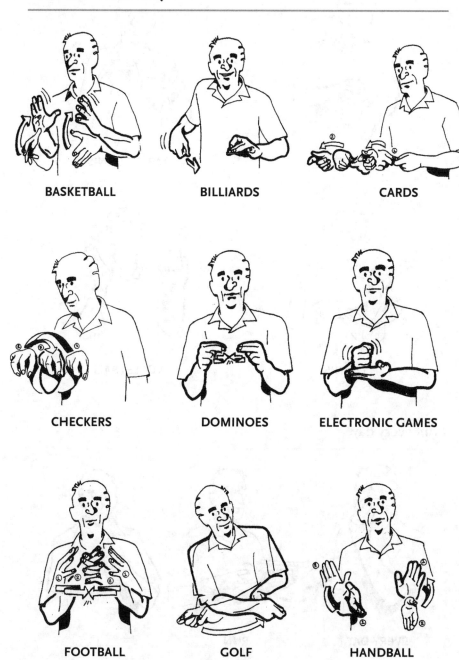

BASKETBALL

BILLIARDS

CARDS

CHECKERS

DOMINOES

ELECTRONIC GAMES

FOOTBALL

GOLF

HANDBALL

SOCCER   TABLE TENNIS

TENNIS   VOLLEYBALL

I run every day.

EVERY DAY   RUN   I

I enjoy going to the mountains to fish.

MOUNTAIN GO TO FISHING PLEASE

Can you ski?

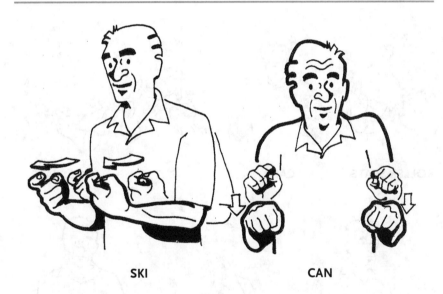

SKI CAN

I went camping last summer.

PAST   SUMMER   TENT   I

I can roller-skate, but I've never tried ice-skating.

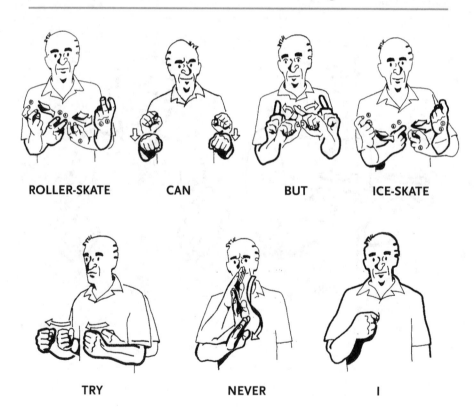

ROLLER-SKATE   CAN   BUT   ICE-SKATE

TRY   NEVER   I

We went canoeing every day.

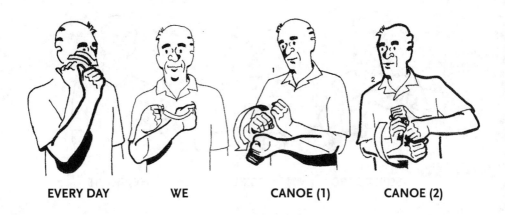

EVERY DAY   WE   CANOE (1)   CANOE (2)

He has a sailboat.

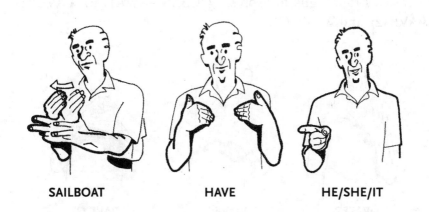

SAILBOAT   HAVE   HE/SHE/IT

She's an expert surfer.

SURFBOARD	**SKILL**	**HE/SHE/IT**

I don't like to swim in the ocean.

It takes four signs to express "OCEAN"—WATER, WAVE (1), WAVE (2), and WAVE (3).

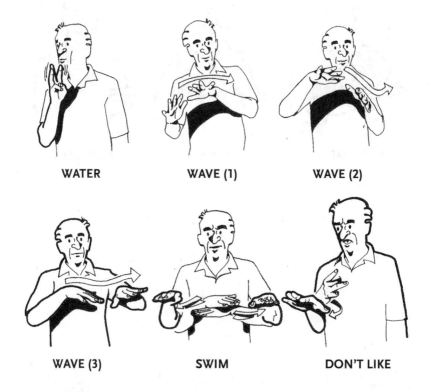

WATER	**WAVE (1)**	**WAVE (2)**
WAVE (3)	**SWIM**	**DON'T LIKE**

Many people hunt in the fall.

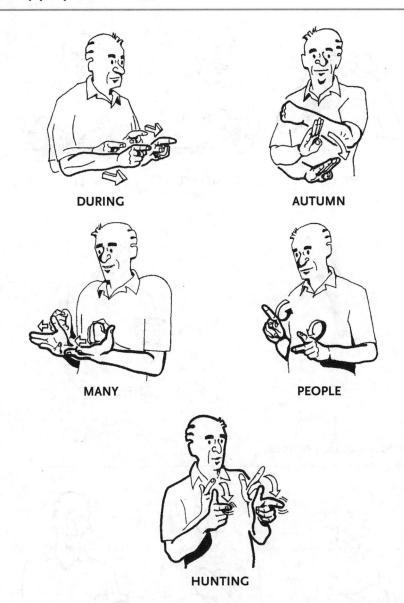

DURING

AUTUMN

MANY

PEOPLE

HUNTING

He's crazy about betting on the horses.

HORSE COMPLETE BET

CRAZY HE/SHE/IT

She loves to ride horses.

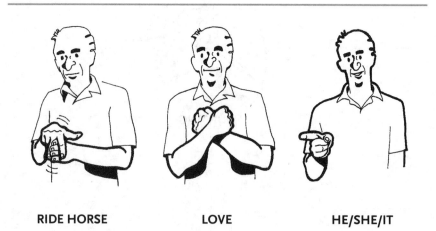

RIDE HORSE LOVE HE/SHE/IT

He hopes to compete in the Olympics.

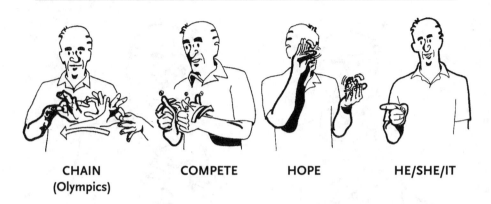

CHAIN
(Olympics)   COMPETE   HOPE   HE/SHE/IT

I hate calisthenics/exercising.

EXERCISE   HATE (1)   HATE (2)   I

What do you do in your spare time?

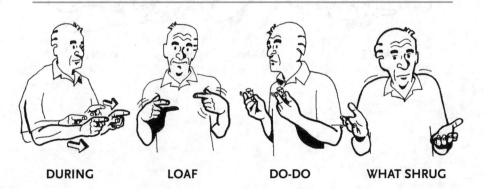

DURING   LOAF   DO-DO   WHAT SHRUG

Do you like to dance?

DANCE   LIKE

Do you want to learn to dance?

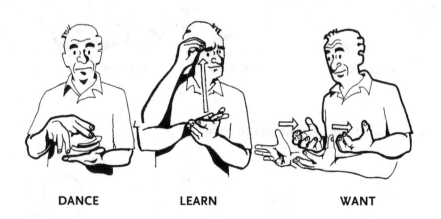

DANCE   LEARN   WANT

Let's stop and rest now.

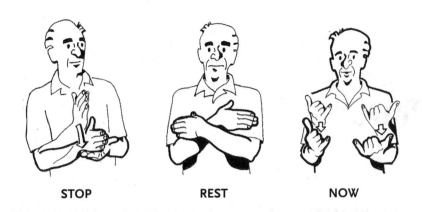

STOP   REST   NOW

I go bowling every week.

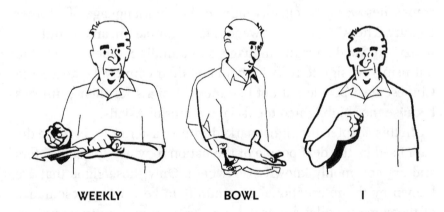

WEEKLY   BOWL   I

13

Travel

In recent years, there has been a movement among U.S. deaf
people to replace ASL signs for other nationalities with the signs
used by the deaf people of those nationalities. The reasons for this
were, first, to show respect for the sign language of those nationalities by using their sign. The second reason was that the ASL sign
sometimes was a derogatory sign in the sign language of another
country. The ASL sign for Sweden, for example, means "drunk" or
"crazy" in Swedish sign language, so naturally Swedes objected to
our using the sign to refer to them and their country. Japanese and
Chinese deaf people did not like the ASL signs for their countries
because they highlighted the facial features of Asians.

In this chapter, the signs marked with an asterisk (*) indicate the
sign used by the deaf people of the nation to which the sign refers
and are commonly known everywhere. Only those signs that are
known by the international community to be truly representative
of the signs used by the deaf people within the country are aster-
isked. (Please keep in mind that not all country signs will be listed
here—instead, a select number will be demonstrated due to space
limitations. I apologize in advance should any reader take offense.)

Areas of the World

Someday I'm going to Africa.

ONLY

DAY

I

GO TO

AFRICA

Additional vocabulary

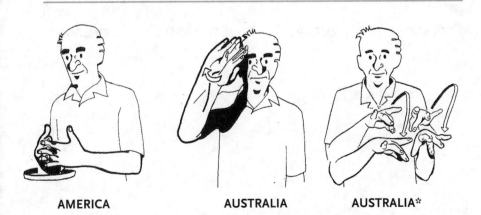

AMERICA

AUSTRALIA

AUSTRALIA*

CANADA   CHINA   CHINA*

DENMARK   DENMARK*   EGYPT

ENGLAND   EUROPE   FINLAND   FINLAND*

FRANCE

GERMANY

GERMANY*

GREECE

HOLLAND

HOLLAND*

INDIA

IRAN*

IRELAND

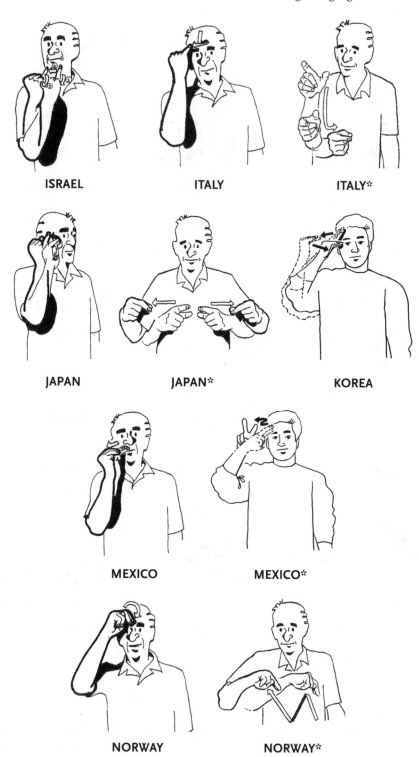

ISRAEL   ITALY   ITALY*

JAPAN   JAPAN*   KOREA

MEXICO   MEXICO*

NORWAY   NORWAY*

POLAND

RUSSIA

SCOTLAND*

SCOTLAND (1)

SCOTLAND (2)

SPAIN

SWEDEN

SWEDEN*

SWITZERLAND

Have you ever been to Japan?

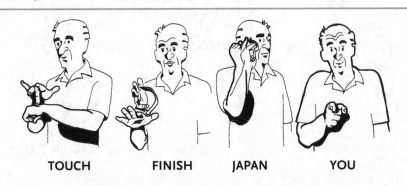

TOUCH

FINISH

JAPAN

YOU

States and Cities of the United States

Almost all states are fingerspelled using the standard written abbreviations such as Penn. or PA, ND, and Wyo. States such as Ohio that have short names are spelled out. The few states that have signs that are used throughout the country are shown below:

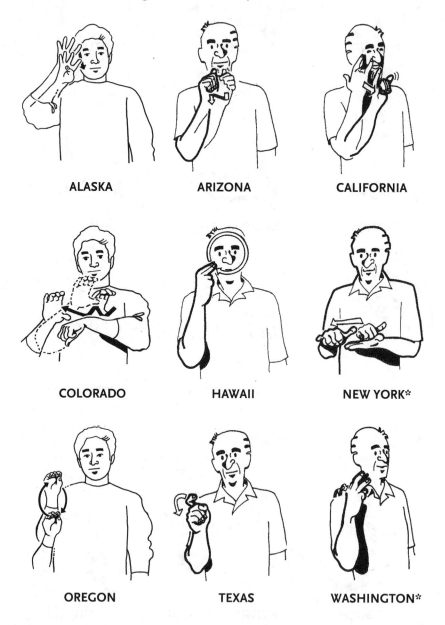

ALASKA   ARIZONA   CALIFORNIA

COLORADO   HAWAII   NEW YORK*

OREGON   TEXAS   WASHINGTON*

*Note that NEW YORK and WASHINGTON can signify the state as well as the city.

I'm flying to New York tonight.

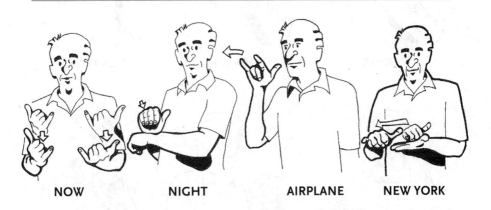

NOW   **NIGHT**   **AIRPLANE**   **NEW YORK**

Almost every city has a sign, or a fingerspelled abbreviation. Often, however, the sign is either not common outside the state or it is the same sign for another city in another state. For example, Berkeley and Boston share the same sign. Therefore, one must inquire of local deaf people how the cities in their state are signed. A few cities do have signs that are used all over the country. New York is one such city, and others are shown on page 248:

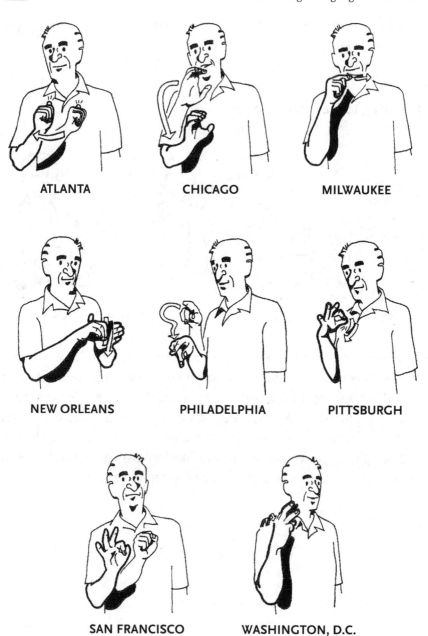

ATLANTA   CHICAGO   MILWAUKEE

NEW ORLEANS   PHILADELPHIA   PITTSBURGH

SAN FRANCISCO   WASHINGTON, D.C.

San Francisco is abbreviated to "SF," and so are many other cities. Take care with Los Angeles, since its abbreviation can also mean Louisiana.

Traveling

Are your bags packed?

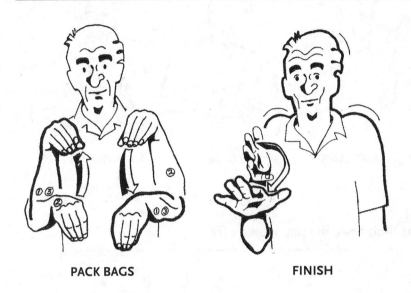

PACK BAGS   FINISH

I'll take you to the airport.

I   BRING   AIRPLANE

Which airline are you taking?

AIRPLANE   NAME   WHICH

What time does the plane take off?

AIRPLANE TAKEOFF   TIME

Do you have your ticket?

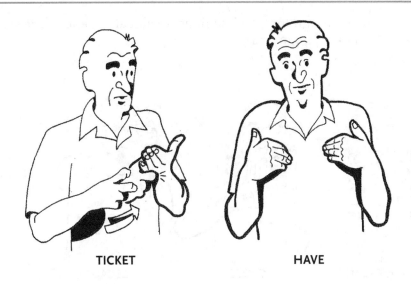

TICKET   HAVE

May I see your ticket, please?

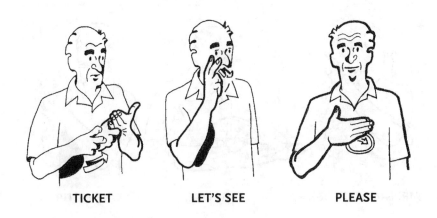

TICKET   LET'S SEE   PLEASE

The airport is closed due to fog.

There is no sign for "fog," so fingerspell it at the end of the sentence, after the sign BECAUSE.

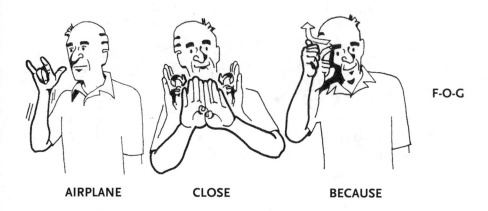

AIRPLANE   CLOSE   BECAUSE   F-O-G

The flight has been delayed an hour.

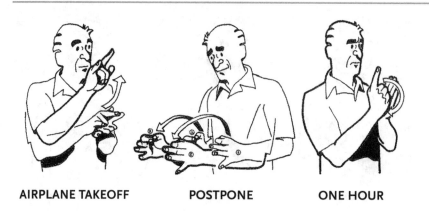

AIRPLANE TAKEOFF   POSTPONE   ONE HOUR

The flight has been canceled.

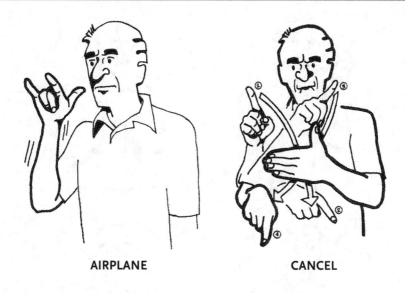

AIRPLANE   CANCEL

I have to change planes in Chicago.

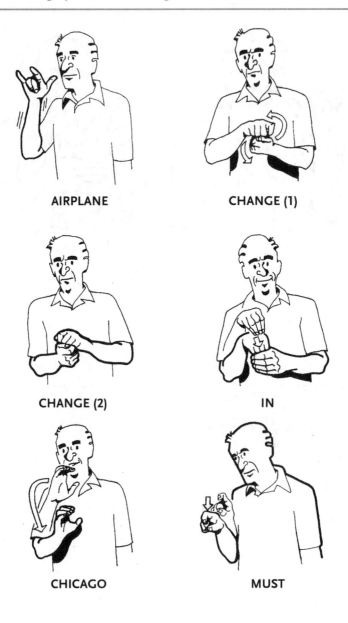

AIRPLANE

CHANGE (1)

CHANGE (2)

IN

CHICAGO

MUST

There's a two-hour layover.

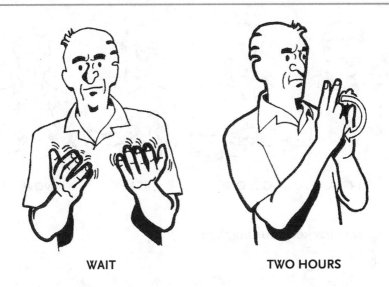

WAIT

TWO HOURS

The seats are not reserved.

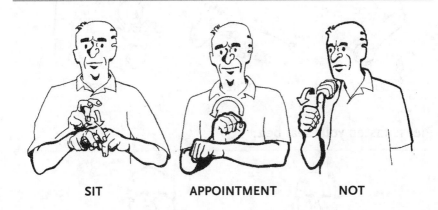

SIT

APPOINTMENT

NOT

The plane is ready for boarding now.

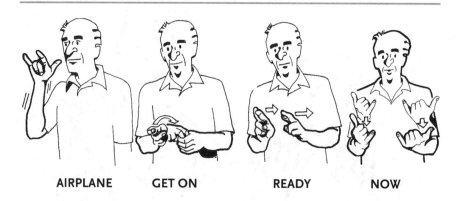

AIRPLANE   GET ON   READY   NOW

Have you checked your luggage?

LUGGAGE   TICKET   FINISH

Please fasten your seat belt.

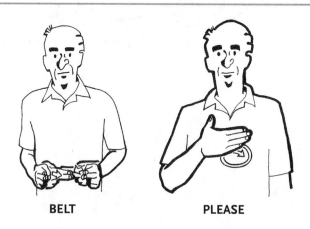

BELT   PLEASE

Would you like a magazine or newspaper?

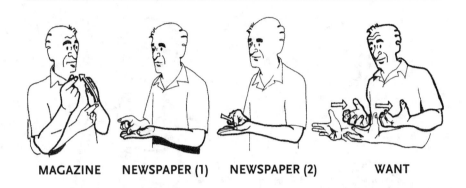

MAGAZINE   NEWSPAPER (1)   NEWSPAPER (2)   WANT

We will land in 10 minutes.

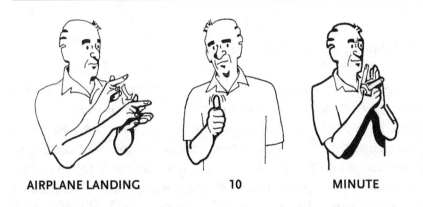

AIRPLANE LANDING   10   MINUTE

Is somebody meeting you?

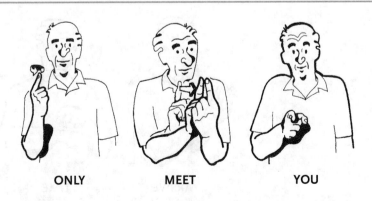

ONLY   MEET   YOU

I enjoy riding the train.

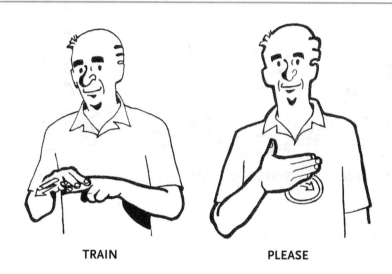

TRAIN   PLEASE

What time does the bus arrive?

A good many languages will share some vocabulary when they come into contact with each other; ASL is one of them. Certain words have been borrowed from the English language and incorporated into the ASL lexicon through a process called *lexicalized fingerspelling*. When this process occurs, many of these fingerspelled words undergo a special transformation and end up looking like a single sign rather than a bunch of letters. In the phrase below, BUS is one example of a lexicalized fingerspelled sign.

B-U-S

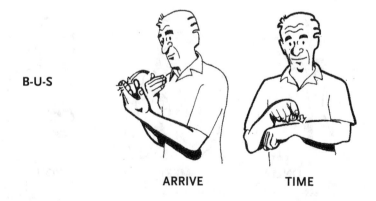

ARRIVE   TIME

What time does the train leave?

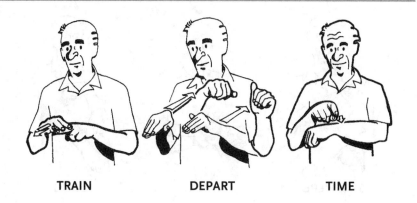

TRAIN   DEPART   TIME

Have you bought your ticket?

TICKET   BUY   FINISH

I'm going to the hotel to take a bath.

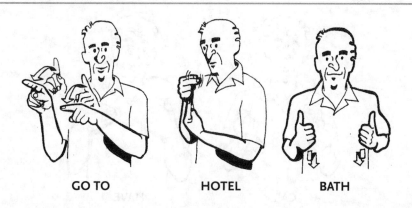

GO TO   HOTEL   BATH

How long are you staying?

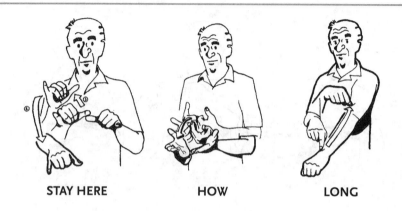

STAY HERE   HOW   LONG

The elevator is stuck.

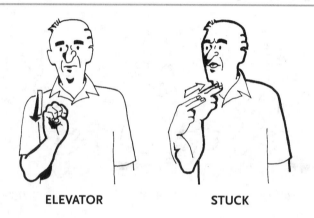

ELEVATOR   STUCK

Do you have a car?

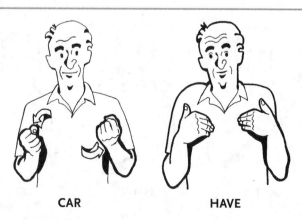

CAR   HAVE

Can you drive?

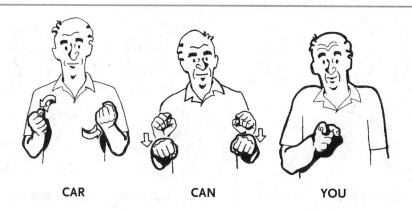

CAR   CAN   YOU

I don't have a license.

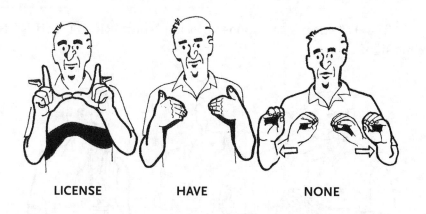

LICENSE   HAVE   NONE

Do you know how to use a manual shift?

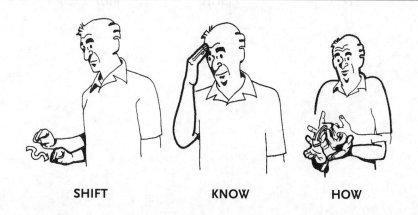

SHIFT   KNOW   HOW

It's illegal to park here overnight.

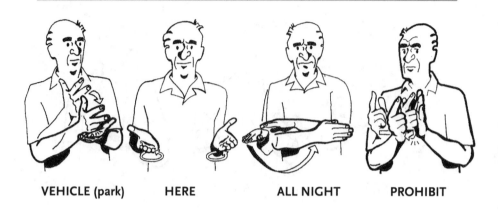

VEHICLE (park) HERE ALL NIGHT PROHIBIT

Slow down and make a right turn.

"RIGHT" means "as opposed to left," but "RIGHT TURN" is one sign.

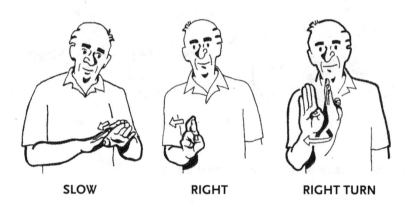

SLOW RIGHT RIGHT TURN

Make a left turn and stop.

"LEFT" means "as opposed to right," but "LEFT TURN" is one sign.

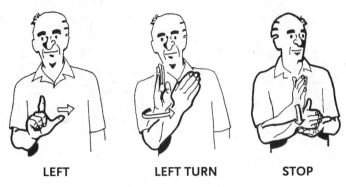

LEFT   LEFT TURN   STOP

Would you call me a cab, please?

The sign CAB is an example of a lexicalized fingerspelling. Fingerspell "cab" at the beginning of the sentence, before the sign PHONE.

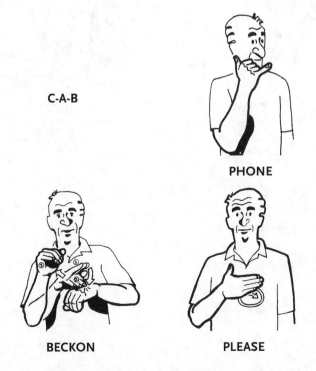

C-A-B

PHONE

BECKON   PLEASE

Come visit me sometime.

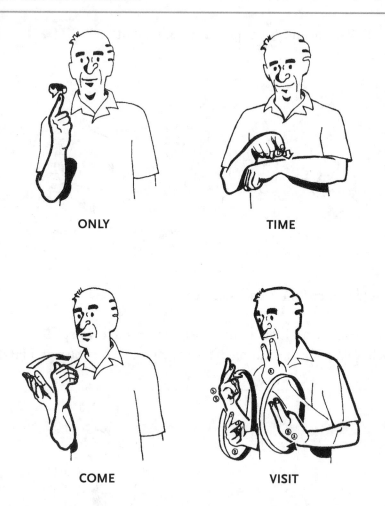

ONLY

TIME

COME

VISIT

14

Animals and Colors

Animals

ASL does not have a sign for every animal. Presented here are nearly all the animal signs that do exist. All other animal names are either fingerspelled or have signs that are known only in a particular area.

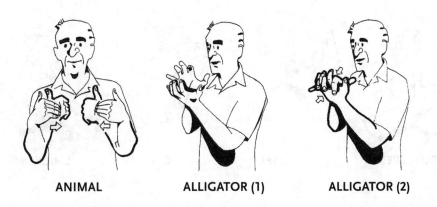

ANIMAL   ALLIGATOR (1)   ALLIGATOR (2)

BEAR (1) BEAR (2) BEE (1)

BEE (2) BIRD (1) BIRD (2)

BUTTERFLY CAMEL CAT CHICKEN*

*While this sign means "chicken," the sign "BIRD" is also often used to mean "chicken."

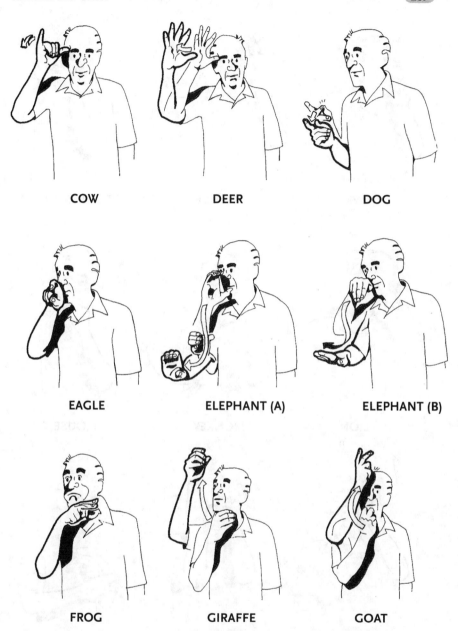

COW DEER DOG

EAGLE ELEPHANT (A) ELEPHANT (B)

FROG GIRAFFE GOAT

HAWK

HORSE

INSECT

LION

MONKEY

MOUSE

MULE

RABBIT (A)

RABBIT (B)

RAT SHEEP SNAKE

TIGER TURKEY (A-1) TURKEY (A-2)

TURKEY (B) WORM

Colors

ASL does not have a sign for every color, so "beige" and "fuchsia" have to be fingerspelled. Colors such as "blue-green," however, may be signed by combining the two signs BLUE and GREEN.

| BLACK | BLUE | BROWN |

| GRAY (1) | GRAY (2) | GREEN |

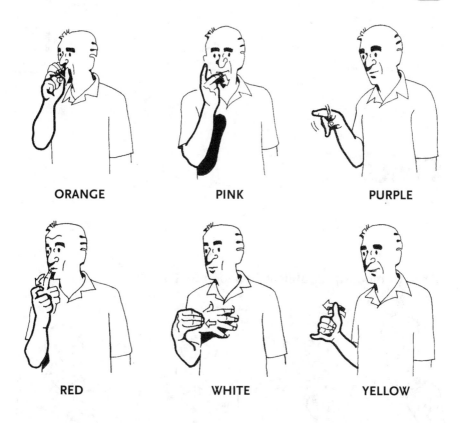

ORANGE   PINK   PURPLE

RED   WHITE   YELLOW

Varying shades of colors can be signed by using the signs DARK and CLEAR. In this sense, CLEAR means "light."

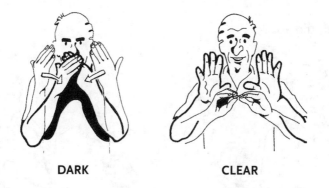

DARK   CLEAR

15

Civics

I'm a Democrat/Republican/Independent.

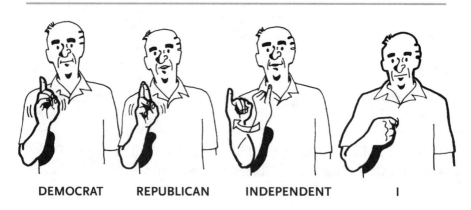

DEMOCRAT   REPUBLICAN   INDEPENDENT   I

I voted; did you?

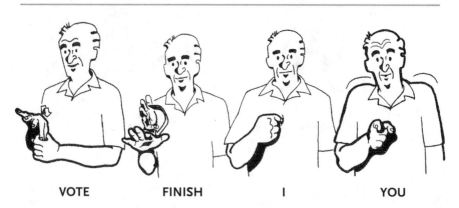

VOTE   FINISH   I   YOU

Who's the new president?

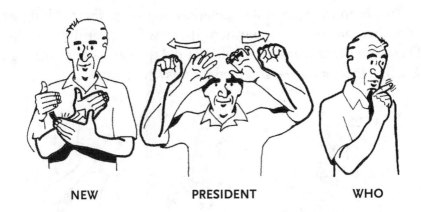

NEW   PRESIDENT   WHO

Who won the election?

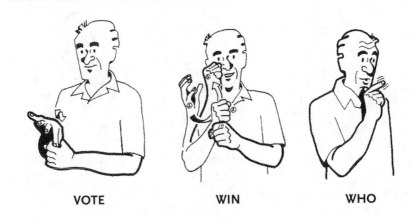

VOTE   WIN   WHO

The legislature/congress is responsible for passing laws.

This is an example of the rhetorical question, where the signer asks, then answers, the question. It is used a great deal in ASL. There is a slight pause at the end of the question—after the sign WHO in this example—and then the answer is signed.

LAW   PASS   RESPONSIBLE

WHO   LEGISLATURE   CONGRESS

She is a congresswoman.

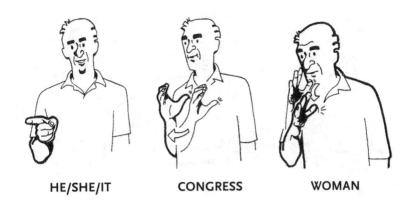

HE/SHE/IT   CONGRESS   WOMAN

He is a senator/governor/judge/lawyer.

The AGENT sign shown below is usually done following the SENATE, GOVERNMENT, JUDGE, and LAW signs to indicate senator, governor, judge, and lawyer, respectively.

HE/SHE/IT   SENATE   GOVERNMENT

JUDGE   LAW   AGENT

We must pay taxes to support the government.

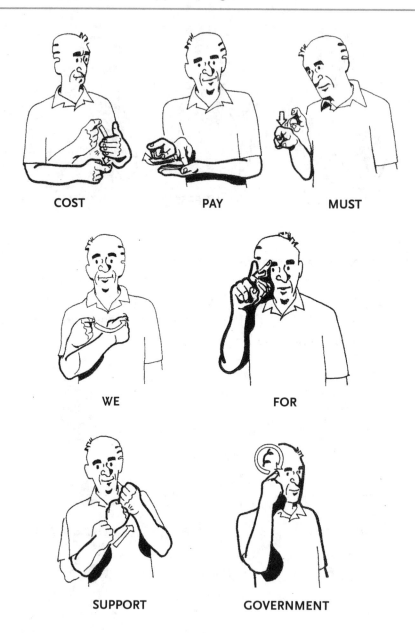

COST   PAY   MUST

WE   FOR

SUPPORT   GOVERNMENT

Our country is large.

Either sign for "country" is acceptable.

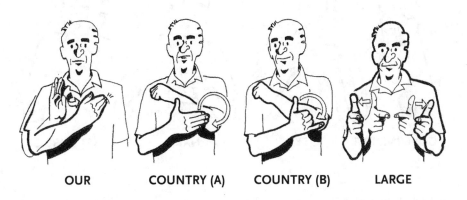

OUR   COUNTRY (A)   COUNTRY (B)   LARGE

I had to pay a parking fine.

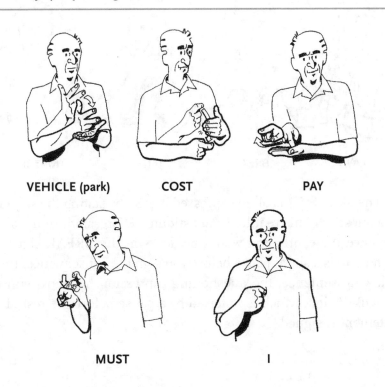

VEHICLE (park)   COST   PAY

MUST   I

Which city is the capital?

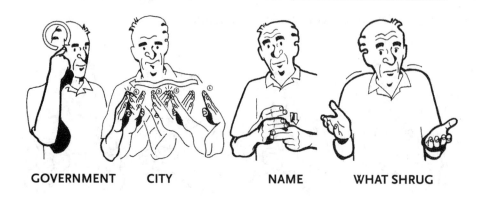

GOVERNMENT   CITY   NAME   WHAT SHRUG

If you break the law, you might go to jail.

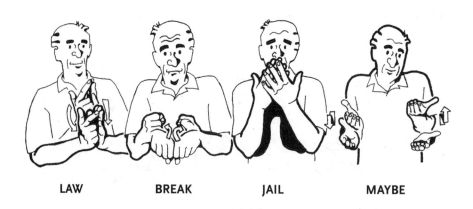

LAW   BREAK   JAIL   MAYBE

The idea of "if" is often expressed in ASL by stating the sentence as a question. This requires a questioning expression. In the above sentence the expression would be done on the BREAK sign, and then there is a slight pause before you sign the consequence. In the following sentence, the questioning expression happens with the DISOBEY sign, which is followed by a pause before the rest of the statement is signed.

If you disobey the law, you will be punished.

LAW   DISOBEY   PUNISH   WILL

You must obey the law.

LAW   OBEY   MUST   YOU

The police arrested him for speeding.

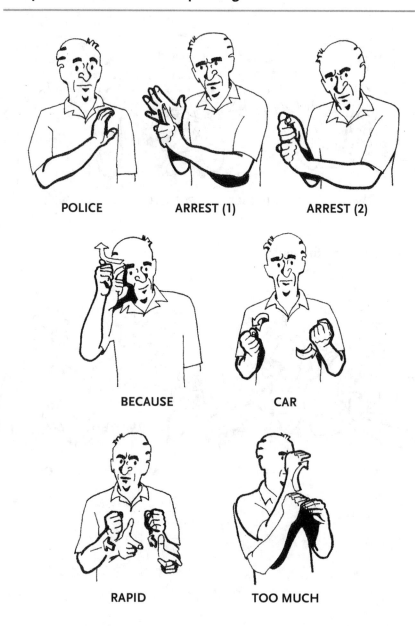

POLICE   ARREST (1)   ARREST (2)

BECAUSE   CAR

RAPID   TOO MUCH

She plans to sue them.

HE/SHE/IT   PLAN   AGAINST

They are on strike against the company.

There is no sign for "company," so fingerspell "C-O" at the end of the sentence after the sign AGAINST.

C-O

THEY   PROTEST   AGAINST

Last year the students protested.

LAST YEAR   **LEARN**   **AGENT**   **PROTEST**

I was on the picket line all morning.

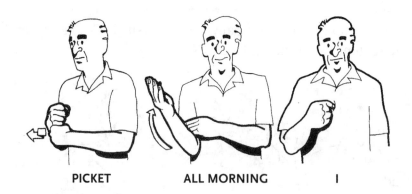

PICKET   **ALL MORNING**   **I**

I move we pass it.

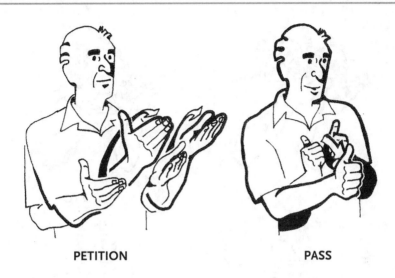

PETITION PASS

I second the motion.

This sign is also used idiomatically to show that you agree with someone.

SECOND A MOTION

Did you receive a notification to appear in court?

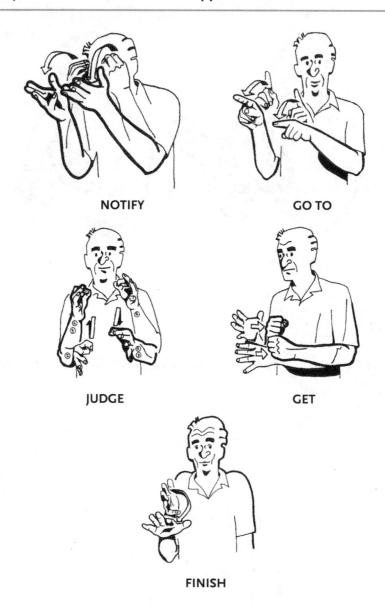

NOTIFY

GO TO

JUDGE

GET

FINISH

Do you belong to the PTA?

There is no sign for "PTA," so fingerspell it at the beginning of the sentence before the sign JOIN.

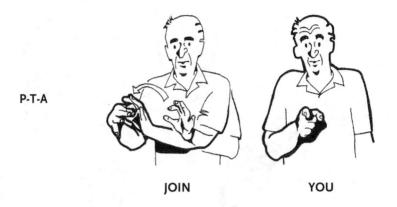

P-T-A

JOIN YOU

He's on Social Security.

Fingerspell "S-S" to indicate "Social Security" at the beginning of the sentence before the sign PENSION.

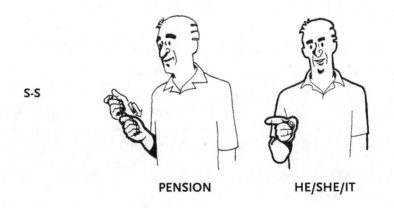

S-S

PENSION HE/SHE/IT

She gets the Supplementary Salary Income.

Fingerspell "S-S-I" to indicate "Supplementary Salary Income" at the beginning of the sentence before the sign PENSION.

S-S-I

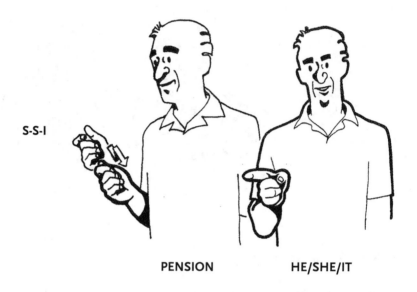

PENSION   HE/SHE/IT

If you go to court, you should have a good lawyer.

Do not forget the questioning facial expression, since this is an "if" statement. It should occur with the sign GO TO.

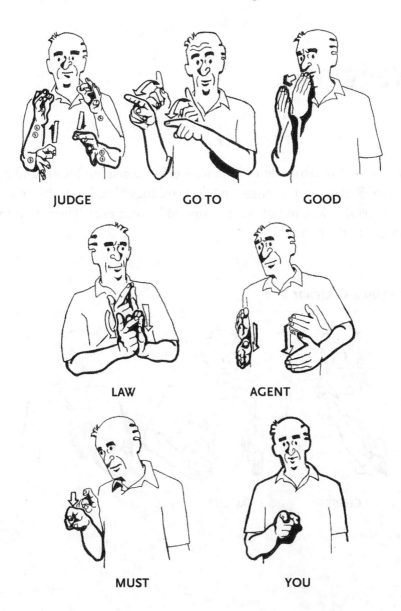

JUDGE   GO TO   GOOD

LAW   AGENT

MUST   YOU

16

Religion

SIGNS FOR VARIOUS denominations differ considerably around the United States, so it is suggested that you make local inquiries about how specific denominations are signed in your area. Those that follow are fairly standard.

Are you a Christian?

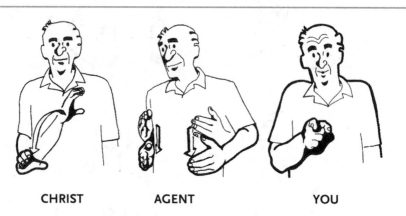

CHRIST   AGENT   YOU

Judaism is an old religion.

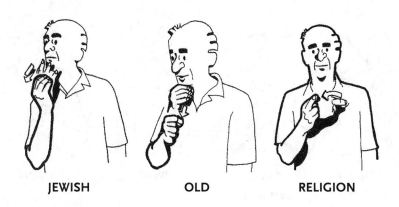

JEWISH   OLD   RELIGION

Note: Although the signs CHERISH and STINGY are very similar, the facial expression is quite different in each case, naturally. The sign JEWISH looks as if you are stroking a beard. It would, obviously, be offensive if you signed STINGY and meant to sign JEWISH, so be careful.

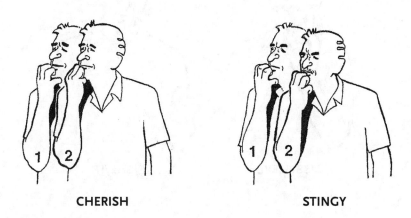

CHERISH   STINGY

Are you a Roman Catholic or a Protestant?

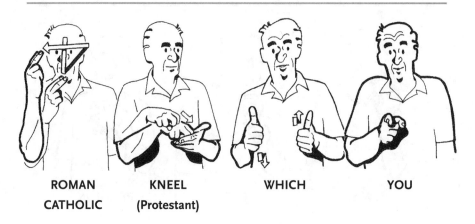

| ROMAN CATHOLIC | KNEEL (Protestant) | WHICH | YOU |

He's an atheist.

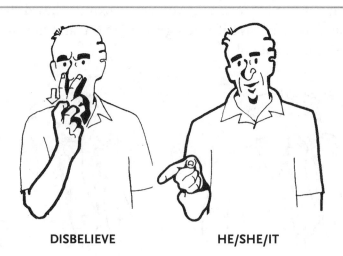

DISBELIEVE   HE/SHE/IT

Additional vocabulary for religious denominations

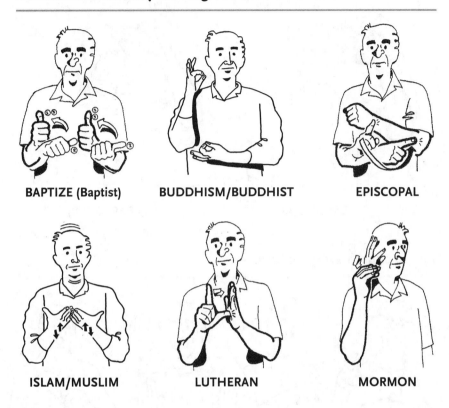

BAPTIZE (Baptist) **BUDDHISM/BUDDHIST** **EPISCOPAL**

ISLAM/MUSLIM **LUTHERAN** **MORMON**

Have you been baptized?

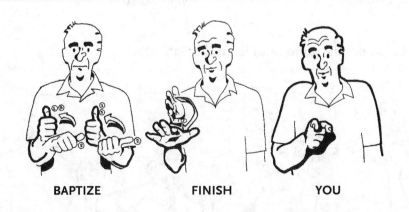

BAPTIZE **FINISH** **YOU**

If a particular denomination baptizes by sprinkling rather than by immersion, then one of the following signs is used:

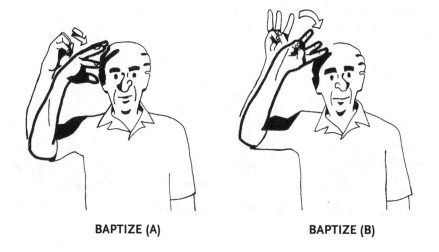

BAPTIZE (A)   BAPTIZE (B)

I go to church every Sunday.

CHURCH   GO TO   EVERY SUNDAY   I

Jewish people go to temple on the Sabbath.

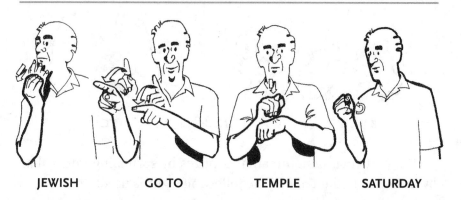

JEWISH   GO TO   TEMPLE   SATURDAY

Which church to you belong to?

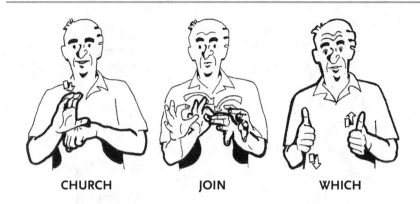

CHURCH   JOIN   WHICH

He used to be a preacher/minister/pastor.

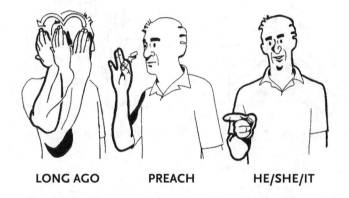

LONG AGO   PREACH   HE/SHE/IT

She's a missionary.

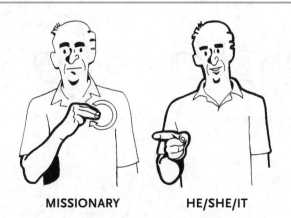

MISSIONARY   HE/SHE/IT

Do you want me to interpret the sermon?

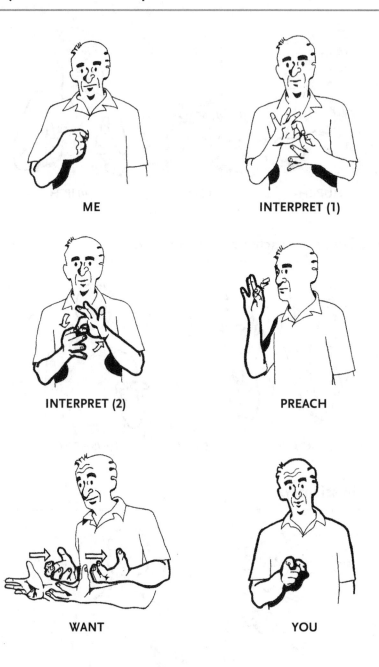

ME

INTERPRET (1)

INTERPRET (2)

PREACH

WANT

YOU

Choir

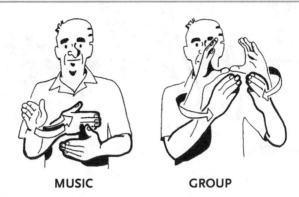

MUSIC   GROUP

Additional vocabulary

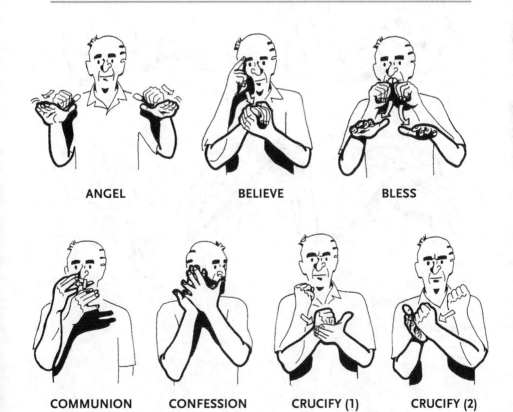

ANGEL   BELIEVE   BLESS

COMMUNION   CONFESSION   CRUCIFY (1)   CRUCIFY (2)

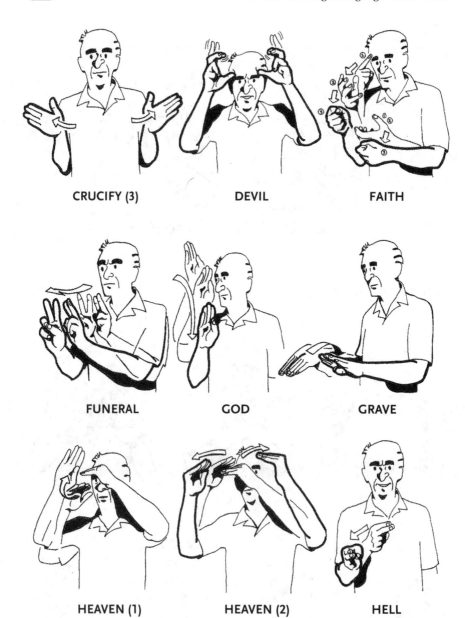

CRUCIFY (3)   DEVIL   FAITH

FUNERAL   GOD   GRAVE

HEAVEN (1)   HEAVEN (2)   HELL

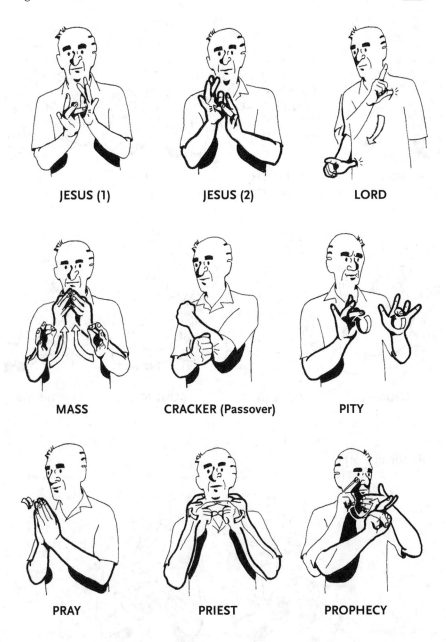

JESUS (1) JESUS (2) LORD

MASS CRACKER (Passover) PITY

PRAY PRIEST PROPHECY

The American Sign Language Phrase Book

| RABBI | SABBATH/ SUNSET | SAVE | SIN |

| SOUL (A) | SOUL (B-1) | SOUL (B-2) | WORSHIP |

Resurrection

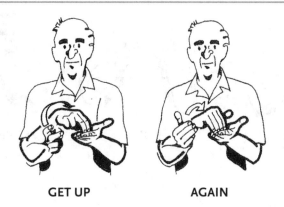

| GET UP | AGAIN |

17

Numbers, Time, Dates, and Money

Numbers

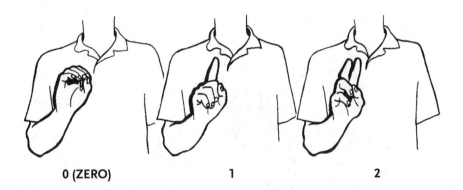

0 (ZERO)   1   2

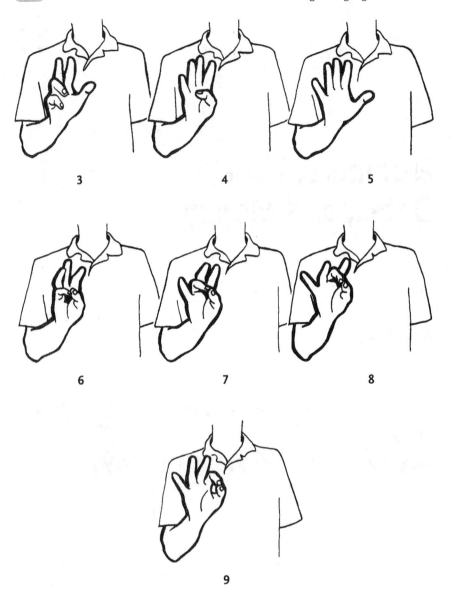

The signs for the number 6 and the letter *W* are exactly the same, and the sign for the number 9 is the same as that for the letter *F*. Context tells you whether the number or the letter is intended.

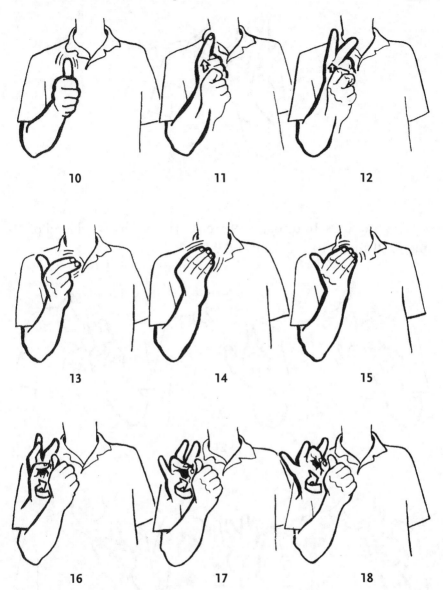

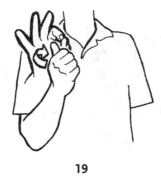

19

The numbers 16 through 19 are actually a very fast blend of 10 and 6, 10 and 7, 10 and 8, 10 and 9.

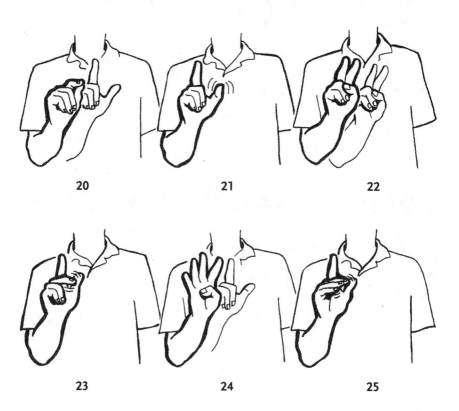

20   21   22

23   24   25

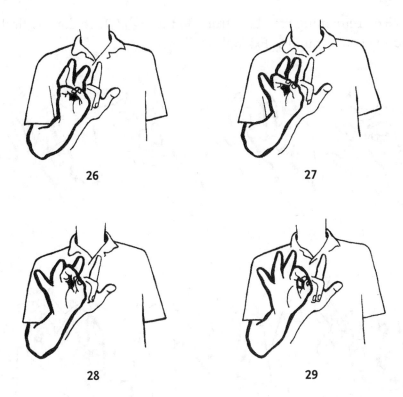

That the "2" in the twenties is made with the thumb and index finger rather than the index and second fingers—as it appears in the number 22—is probably due to the fact that ASL has its roots in the old French sign language. In Europe, even hearing people count *one* with the thumb, and *two* with the thumb and index finger.

The remaining numbers from 30 through 99 are done with the numbers 0 through 9. Examples follow:

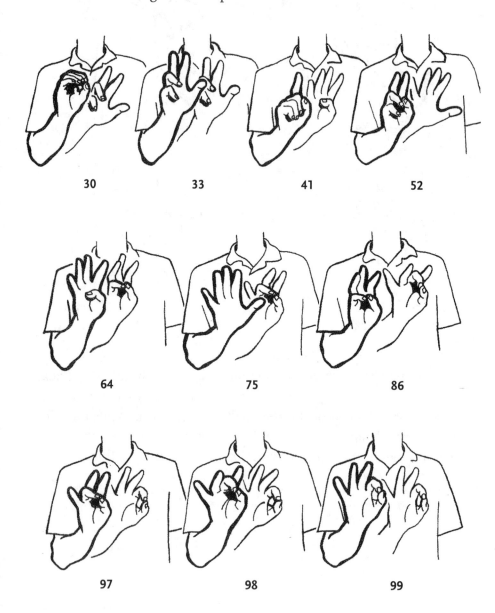

30   33   41   52

64   75   86

97   98   99

The number 100 is made by signing the number 1 and the letter C:

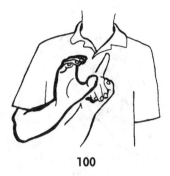

100

The numbers between 100 and 999 are made in one of two ways. One may make the number "7-7-7" or one may sign "7-C-7-7":

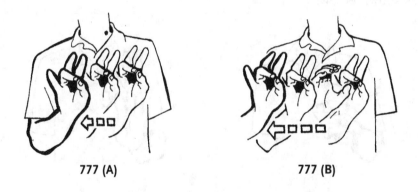

777 (A)   **777 (B)**

The numbers 1,000 and 1,000,000 are signed like so:

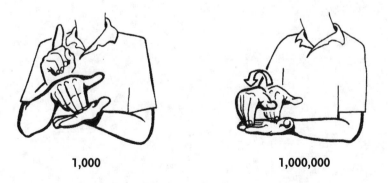

1,000   **1,000,000**

The numbers "billion" and "trillion" are fingerspelled—there is not a specific sign for them.

Fractions are made the same way they are written, one number above another:

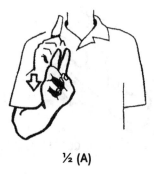

½ (A)

The one-half sign as shown above is usually made more quickly as shown below:

½ (B)

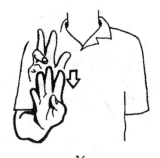

¾

Percentages are made as follows:

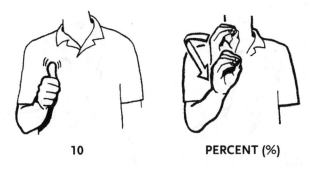

10   PERCENT (%)

Numbers with decimals can also be expressed:

1-.7-5

The sign for the decimal may also mean the punctuation mark "period."

What's your number?

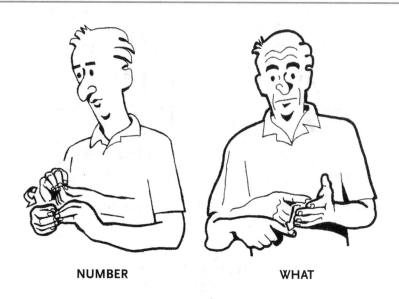

NUMBER   WHAT

My phone number is _____.

Fingerspell your phone number after the sign NUMBER.

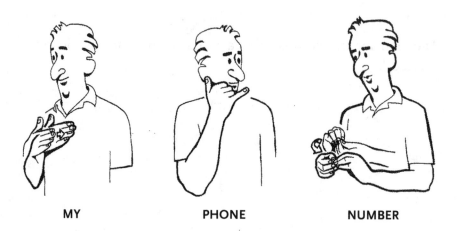

MY   PHONE   NUMBER

Time

Telling time in ASL is usually done exactly in the same way as it is done in English.

It is 4:45.

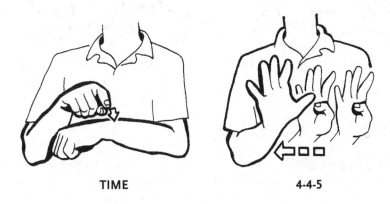

TIME   4-4-5

It is 6:15.

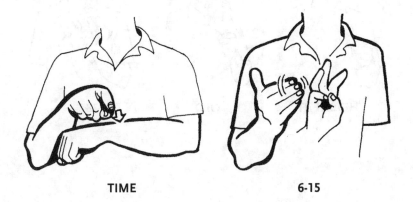

TIME   6-15

It is ten till nine.

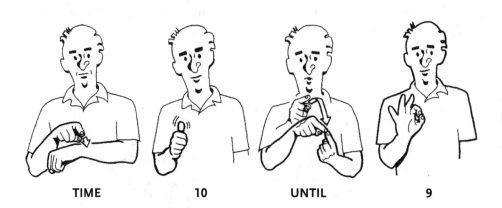

| TIME | 10 | UNTIL | 9 |

Dates

He is 87 years old.

| HE/SHE/IT | OLD | 87 |

I was born in 1911.

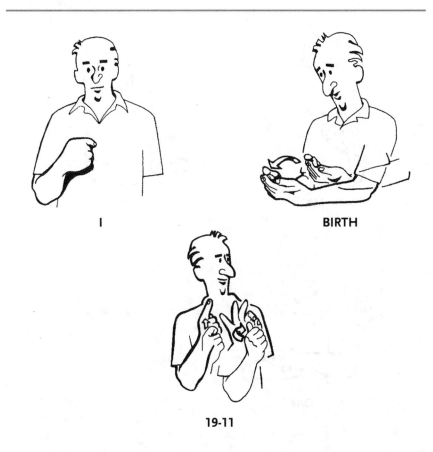

I

BIRTH

19-11

Most of the months are abbreviated in fingerspelling. Only the short ones—March, April, May, June, and July—are spelled out completely.

My birthday is April 3, 1948.

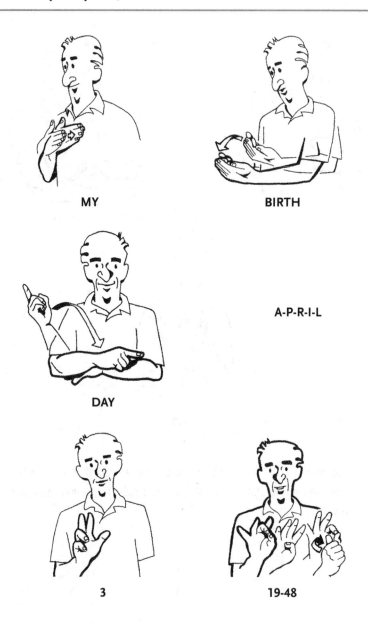

MY

BIRTH

A-P-R-I-L

DAY

3

19-48

Additional vocabulary

MONDAY   TUESDAY   WEDNESDAY

THURSDAY   FRIDAY   SATURDAY

WONDERFUL
(Sunday)   WEEK   LAST WEEK

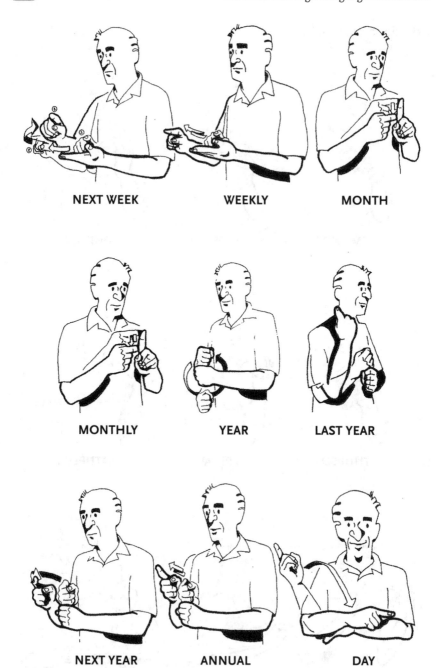

NEXT WEEK   **WEEKLY**   **MONTH**

MONTHLY   **YEAR**   **LAST YEAR**

NEXT YEAR   **ANNUAL**   **DAY**

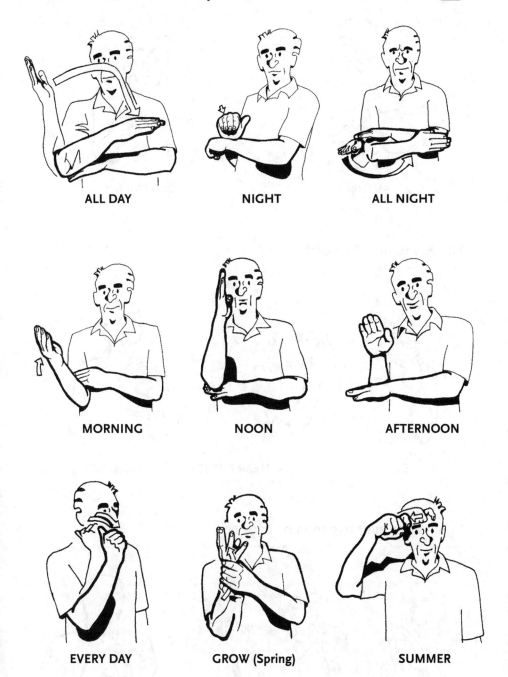

ALL DAY

NIGHT

ALL NIGHT

MORNING

NOON

AFTERNOON

EVERY DAY

GROW (Spring)

SUMMER

AUTUMN

COLD (Winter)

I'll see you next Monday.

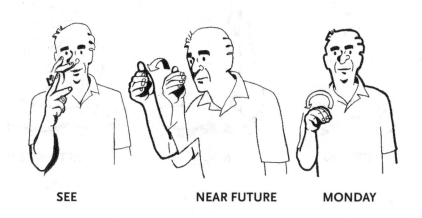

SEE **NEAR FUTURE** **MONDAY**

I visited my aunt two months ago.

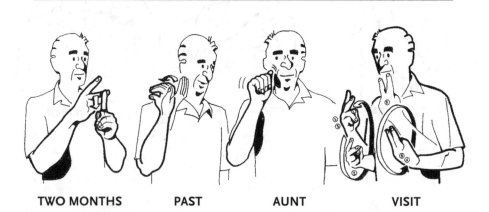

TWO MONTHS **PAST** **AUNT** **VISIT**

I bought a new house two years ago.

TWO YEARS AGO BUY NEW HOUSE

I graduate in two years.

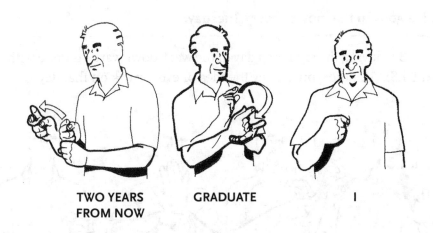

TWO YEARS FROM NOW GRADUATE I

I pay every three months.

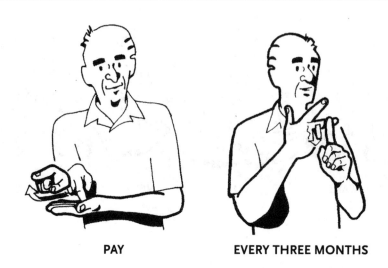

PAY — EVERY THREE MONTHS

He goes to the movies every Tuesday.

By moving the sign for a day of the week downward, as done with TUESDAY here, you convey the idea of every week on that day.

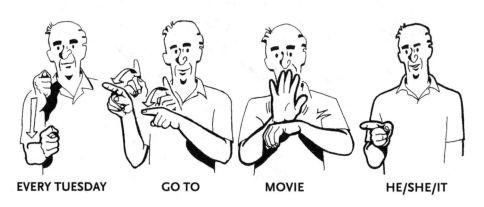

EVERY TUESDAY — GO TO — MOVIE — HE/SHE/IT

I see her every Saturday.

EVERY SATURDAY   SEE

The Fourth of July is a holiday.

Fingerspell JULY at the beginning of the sentence before the sign 4TH.

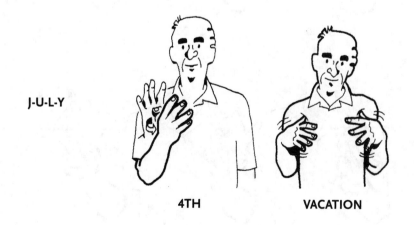

J-U-L-Y

4TH   VACATION

Money

These signs also serve as ordinal numbers—i.e., first, second, third, etc.

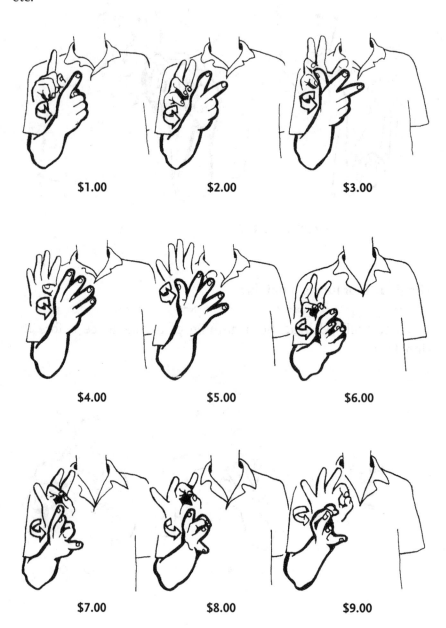

$1.00	$2.00	$3.00
$4.00	$5.00	$6.00
$7.00	$8.00	$9.00

The sign DOLLAR is used when the amount is over nine dollars or when speaking specifically of a bill, as in "a dollar bill." As here:

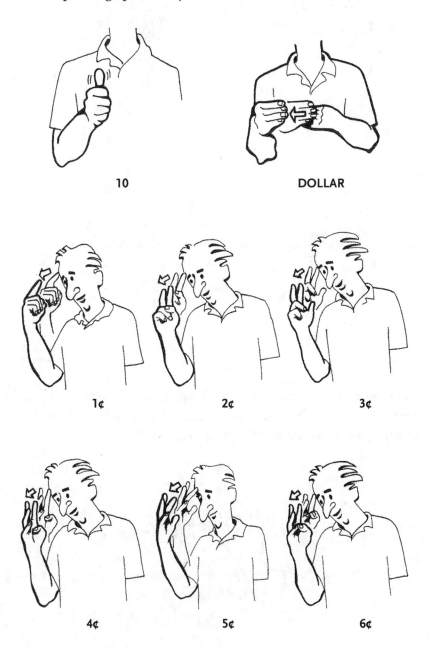

10   DOLLAR

1¢   2¢   3¢

4¢   5¢   6¢

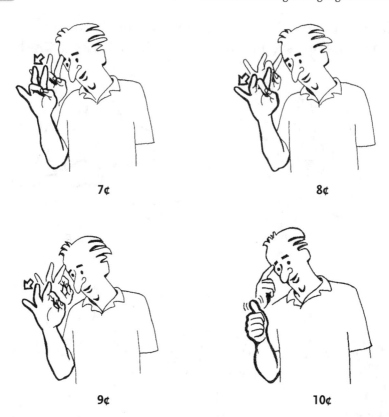

7¢   8¢

9¢   10¢

These signs are used only when speaking of these amounts by themselves, not when they are preceded by a dollar amount. For example, $3.09 would be signed as follows:

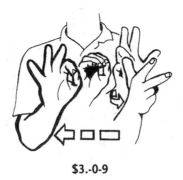

$3.-0-9

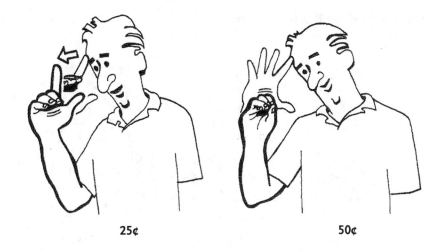

25¢   50¢

The same applies to the following two signs as to the cent signs above. Use them only when speaking of these amounts alone, and not with a dollar amount.

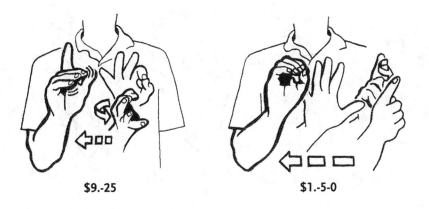

$9.-25 $1.-5-0

How much does the book cost?

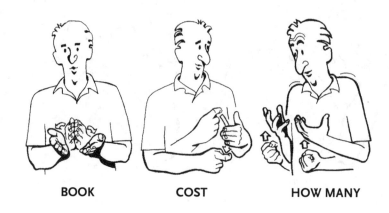

BOOK   COST   HOW MANY

Have you a nickel/dime/quarter?

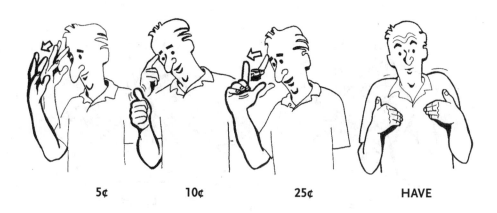

5¢   10¢   25¢   HAVE

Can you change a five?

$5.00   SHARE (make change)   CAN

How much did you pay?

PAY   HOW MANY

It's under five dollars.

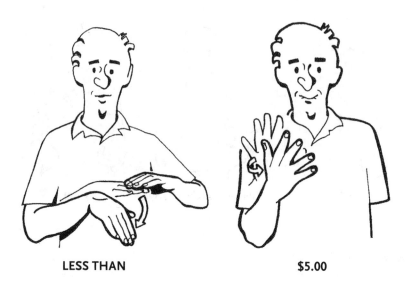

LESS THAN $5.00

It's over five dollars.

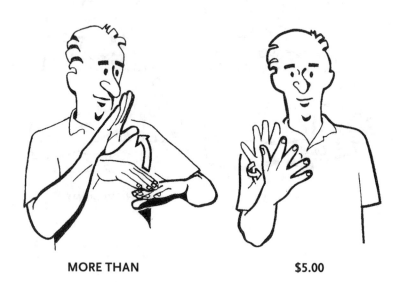

MORE THAN $5.00

I paid less than you.

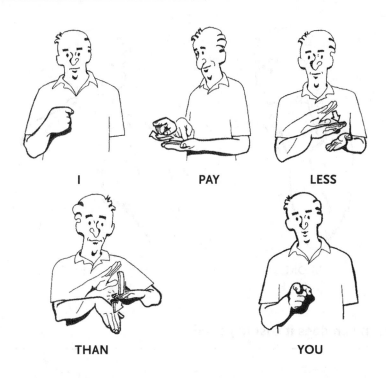

I   PAY   LESS

THAN   YOU

I have no money.

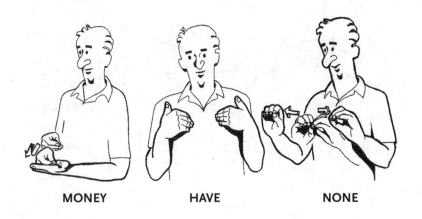

MONEY   HAVE   NONE

I'm broke.

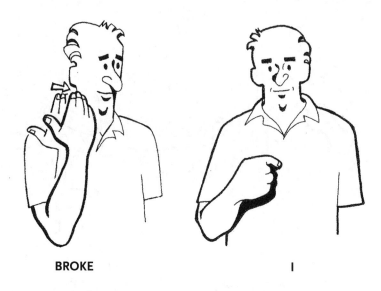

BROKE   I

How much does it cost to get in?

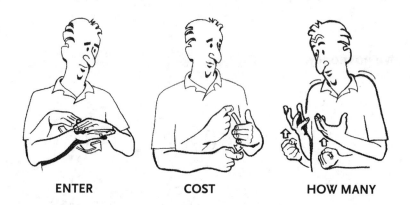

ENTER   COST   HOW MANY

How much does he owe?

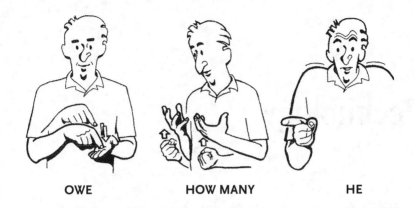

OWE   HOW MANY   HE

18

Technology

Pᴌᴇᴀsᴇ ɴᴏᴛᴇ ᴛʜᴀᴛ this chapter illustrates several variations of the word *computer,* as commonly used by deaf people.

I have e-mail.

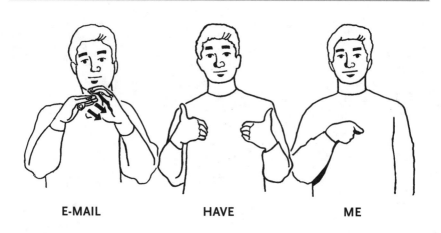

E-MAIL   HAVE   ME

Would you mind giving me your e-mail address?

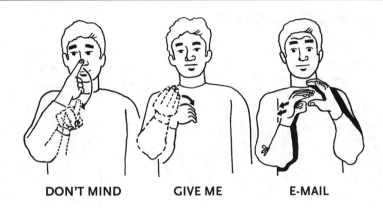

DON'T MIND   GIVE ME   E-MAIL

Which Internet service provider do you use? AOL or MSN?

Fingerspell "A-O-L" and "M-S-N."

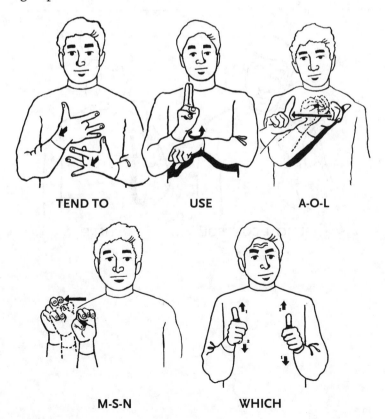

TEND TO   USE   A-O-L

M-S-N   WHICH

Do you have cable TV?

Fingerspell TV and CABLE.

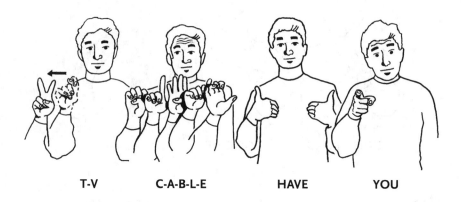

| T-V | C-A-B-L-E | HAVE | YOU |

Where's the remote?

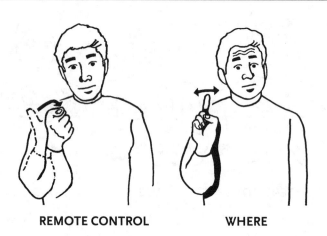

| REMOTE CONTROL | WHERE |

I do not have cable service.

Fingerspell CABLE.

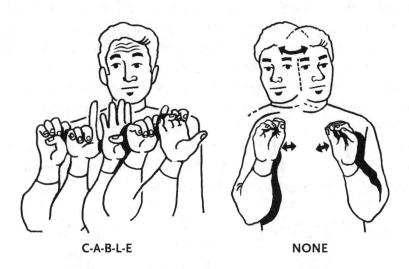

C-A-B-L-E   NONE

He/she has a high-definition TV.

Fingerspell "H-D T-V."

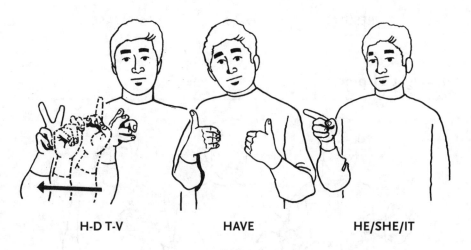

H-D T-V   HAVE   HE/SHE/IT

Please fax me your résumé.

Fingerspell FAX. *Fax* is another example of a word borrowed from English through the lexicalized fingerspelling process that has taken on the appearance of a single sign. With frequent usage, signers have added movement, dropped letters, or altered palm orientation to certain lexicalized fingerspelled signs, which is the case with the word *fax*. The letters "F" and "X" move toward the signer's chest, the letter "A" has been dropped, and the palm orientation of the letter "X" has been shifted toward the signer's chest. Lexicalized fingerspelled words do not follow the rules of regularly fingerspelled words (e.g., P-T-A, D-V-D, S-S-I). Refer to the Appendix for more information on the manual alphabet.

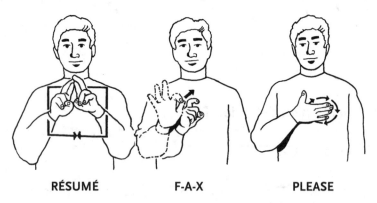

RÉSUMÉ   F-A-X   PLEASE

I bought a laptop.

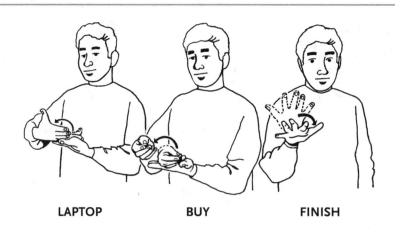

LAPTOP   BUY   FINISH

What make is your computer?

COMPUTER   YOUR   NAME

How much memory does your computer have?

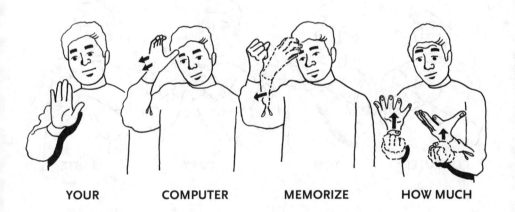

YOUR   COMPUTER   MEMORIZE   HOW MUCH

I don't have high-speed Internet access.

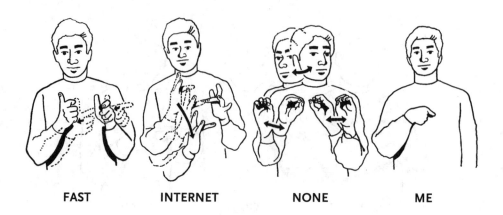

| FAST | INTERNET | NONE | ME |

Copy and paste your document.

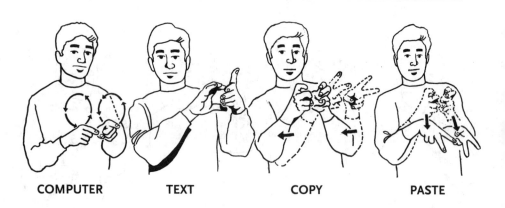

| COMPUTER | TEXT | COPY | PASTE |

Download this program.

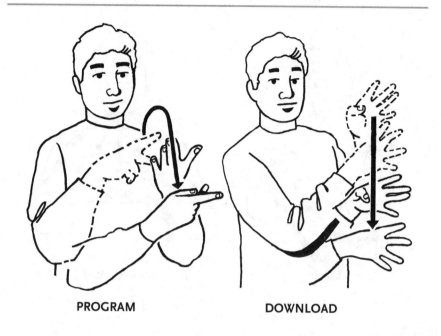

PROGRAM   DOWNLOAD

Have you printed your document?

PAPER   PRINT   FINISH

My printer is broken.

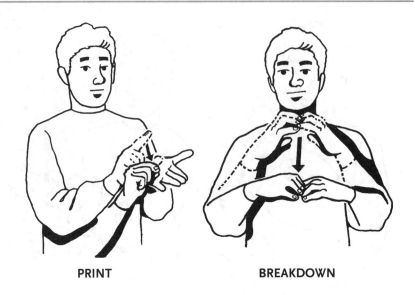

PRINT   BREAKDOWN

Please save your file.

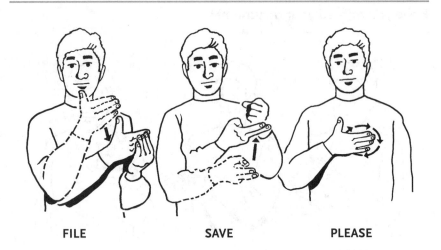

FILE   SAVE   PLEASE

I accidentally deleted my file.

Note: You can use either the MISTAKE or CARELESS sign with this phrase.

FILE   **DELETE**   **MISTAKE**   or   **CARELESS**

Did you scan your photograph?

Note: You can use either version of SCAN for this phrase.

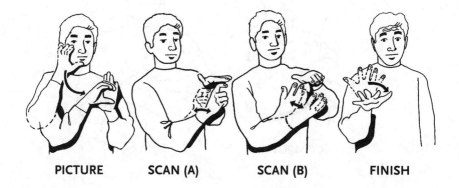

PICTURE   **SCAN (A)**   **SCAN (B)**   **FINISH**

Send your picture as an attachment.

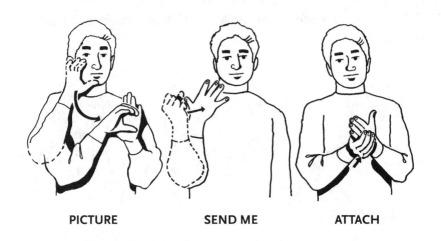

PICTURE   SEND ME   ATTACH

My computer crashed!

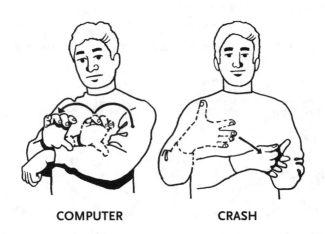

COMPUTER   CRASH

A virus destroyed my hard drive.

Fingerspell "H-D" and VIRUS.

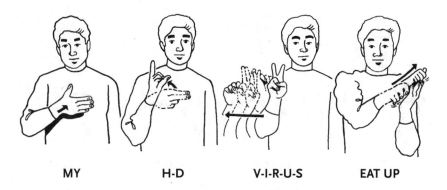

| MY | H-D | V-I-R-U-S | EAT UP |

Which software do you prefer?

Software is another example of the lexicalized fingerspelling process becoming like a sign. The word has been shortened or abbreviated to the letters "S" and "W." The sign movement starts with the palm orientation of the letter "S" reversed inward toward the signer's chest. The "S" palm orientation swings outward away from the signer and the next letter, "W," is fingerspelled.

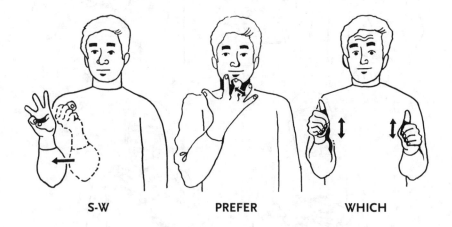

| S-W | PREFER | WHICH |

Please burn a CD.

Fingerspell "C-D."

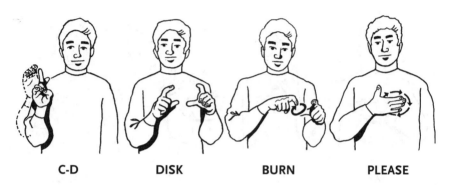

| C-D | DISK | BURN | PLEASE |

I will buy a DVD/VHS player.

Fingerspell "D-V-D" and "V-H-S."

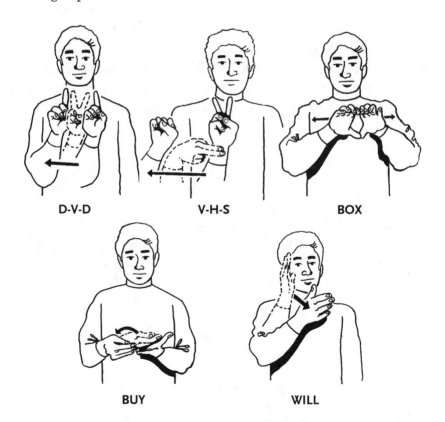

| D-V-D | V-H-S | BOX |

| BUY | WILL |

A satellite dish is expensive!

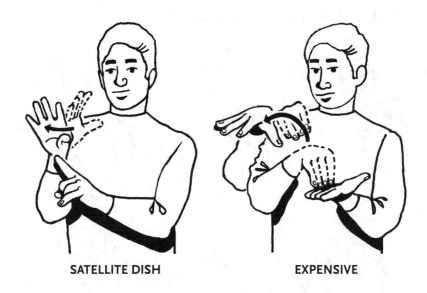

SATELLITE DISH　　　　　　　EXPENSIVE

My camcorder works fine.

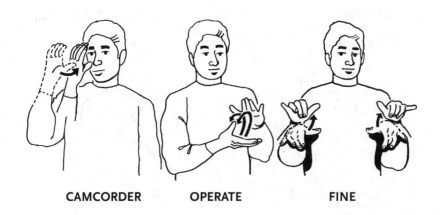

CAMCORDER　　　OPERATE　　　FINE

My parents gave me a 35-mm digital camera for my birthday.

"M-M" and DIGITAL are fingerspelled.

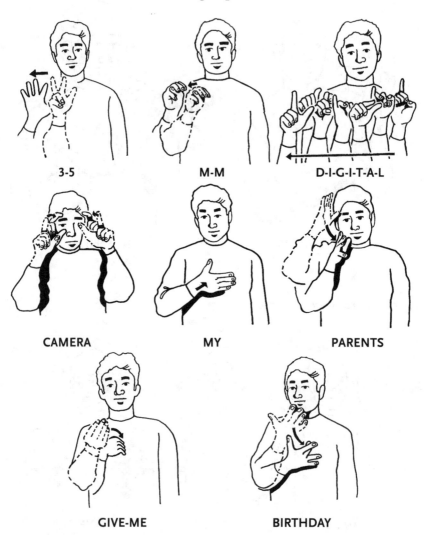

3-5   M-M   D-I-G-I-T-A-L

CAMERA   MY   PARENTS

GIVE-ME   BIRTHDAY

My aunt got a GPS for her boat.

Fingerspell "G-P-S." This is an example of a rhetorical question where the signer asks, and then answers, the question. It is used a great deal in ASL. There is a slight pause at the end of the question—after the sign FOR-FOR in this example—and then the answer is signed.

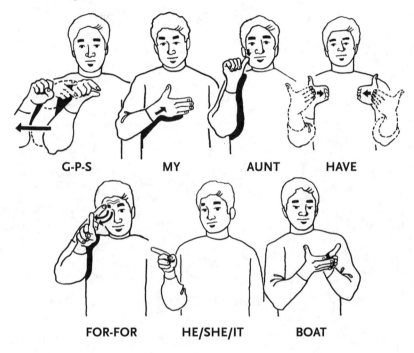

G-P-S   MY   AUNT   HAVE

FOR-FOR   HE/SHE/IT   BOAT

iPods are very popular!

Fingerspell IPOD.

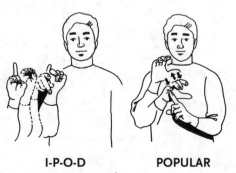

I-P-O-D   POPULAR

That coffeehouse doesn't have wi-fi access.

Fingerspell WI-FI.

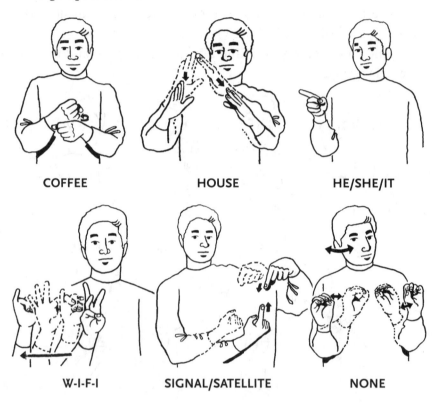

COFFEE   HOUSE   HE/SHE/IT

W-I-F-I   SIGNAL/SATELLITE   NONE

What's the link to that blog?

Fingerspell BLOG.

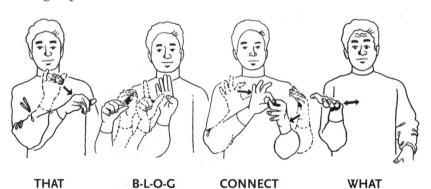

THAT   B-L-O-G   CONNECT   WHAT

This theater downtown has open captioning.

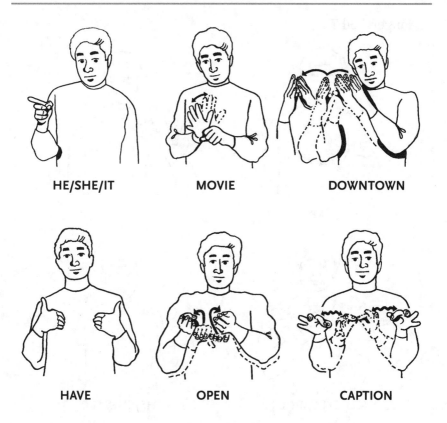

HE/SHE/IT   MOVIE   DOWNTOWN

HAVE   OPEN   CAPTION

My TV has closed captioning.

Fingerspell TV.

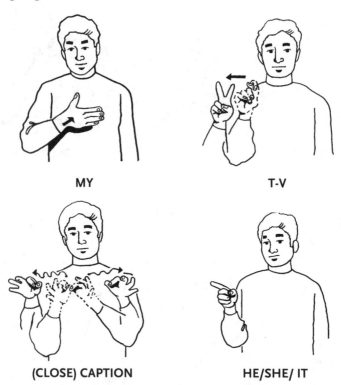

MY   T-V

(CLOSE) CAPTION   HE/SHE/ IT

Which pager did you choose?

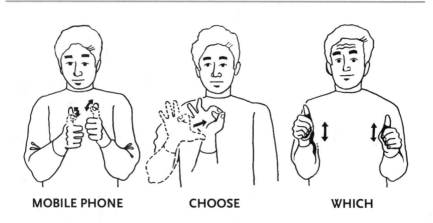

MOBILE PHONE   CHOOSE   WHICH

I need to recharge my pager.

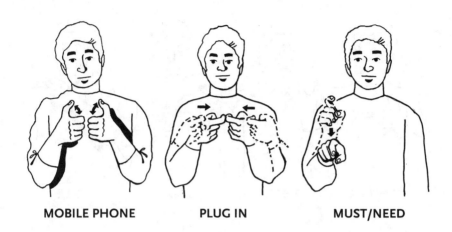

MOBILE PHONE   PLUG IN   MUST/NEED

Mine's a BlackBerry pager.

Fingerspell "B-B."

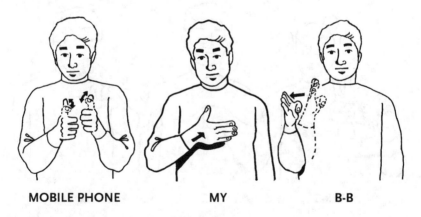

MOBILE PHONE   MY   B-B

I will buy a Sidekick III pager.

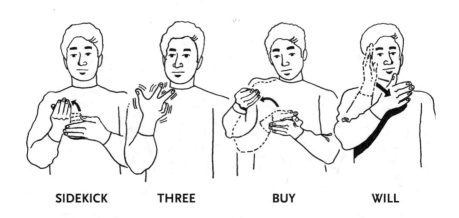

SIDEKICK   THREE   BUY   WILL

I love video relay service!

Fingerspell "V-R-S."

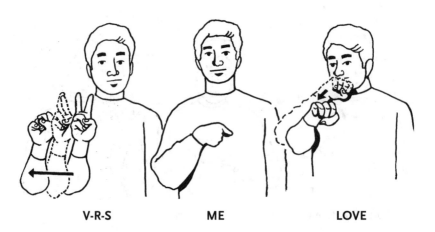

V-R-S   ME   LOVE

A few people use the voice carryover feature on the video relay service.

Fingerspell "V-R-S."

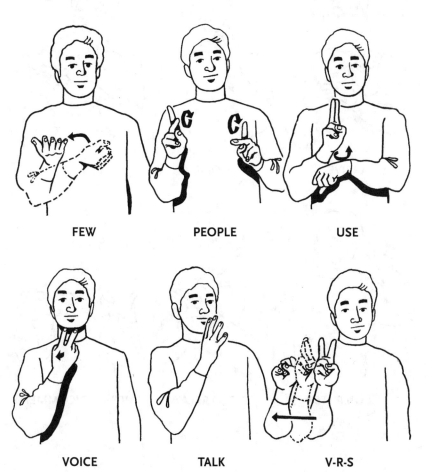

FEW	PEOPLE	USE
VOICE	TALK	V-R-S

When you get home, check your video relay mail.

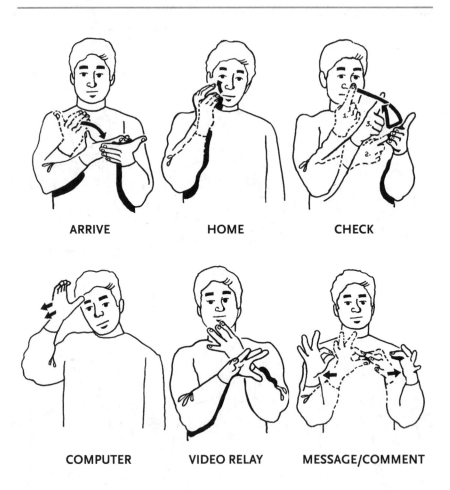

ARRIVE HOME CHECK

COMPUTER VIDEO RELAY MESSAGE/COMMENT

The wireless Internet relay on my pager is terrific!

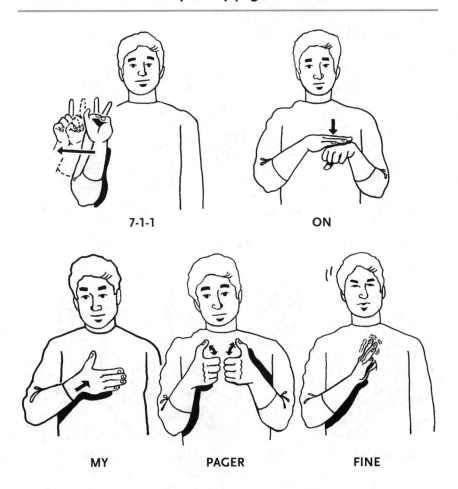

7-1-1   ON

MY   PAGER   FINE

Sometimes I use the IP relay on my computer.

Fingerspell "I-P" and RELAY.

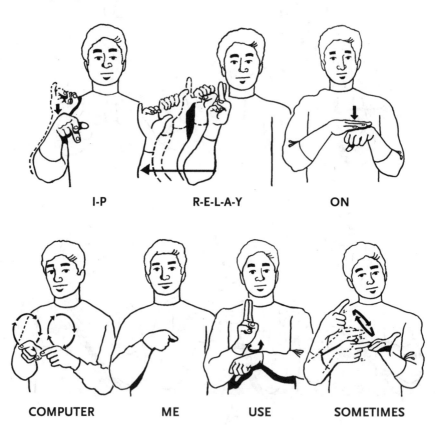

I-P   R-E-L-A-Y   ON

COMPUTER   ME   USE   SOMETIMES

Deaf people text message their hearing friends.

Fingerspell TEXT.

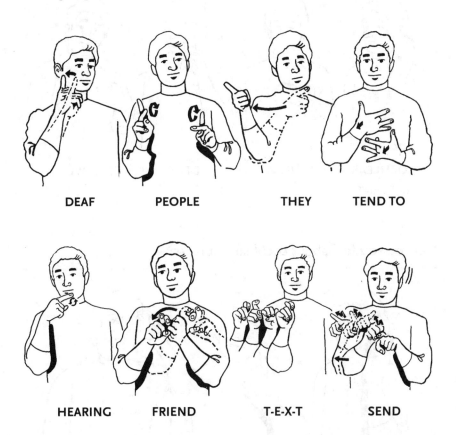

DEAF	PEOPLE	THEY	TEND TO

HEARING	FRIEND	T-E-X-T	SEND

Some deaf people have gotten cochlear implants.

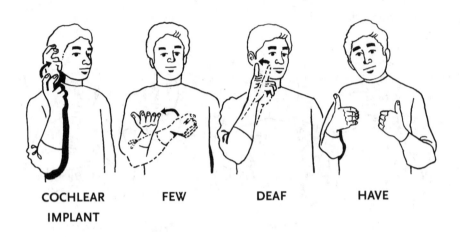

| COCHLEAR IMPLANT | FEW | DEAF | HAVE |

How do you feel about cochlear implants?

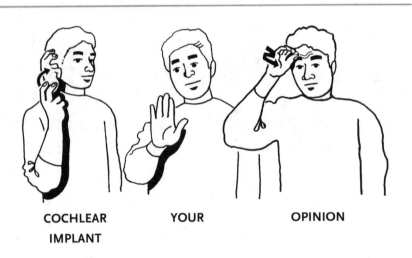

| COCHLEAR IMPLANT | YOUR | OPINION |

My deaf-blind friend has a closed-circuit television magnifier.

Fingerspell "C-C-T-V."

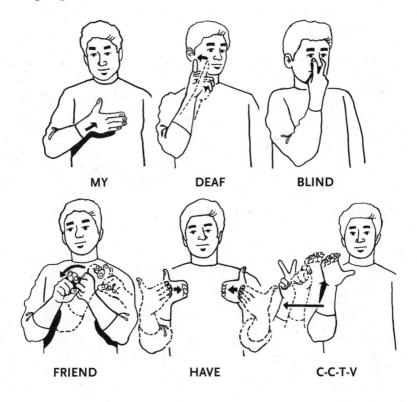

MY   DEAF   BLIND

FRIEND   HAVE   C-C-T-V

Did you see that vlog?

Fingerspell VLOG.

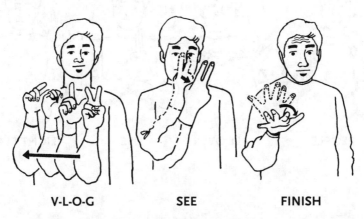

V-L-O-G   SEE   FINISH

Most deaf people use light-signaling devices for their doorbells, alarm clocks, videophones, and TTYs, and to alert them to a baby's cry.

Fingerspell "T-T-Y."

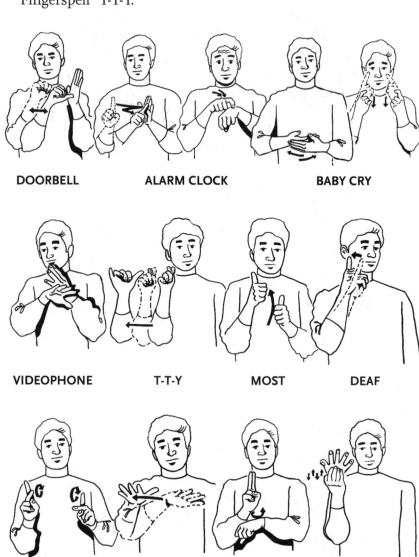

DOORBELL   ALARM CLOCK   BABY CRY

VIDEOPHONE   T-T-Y   MOST   DEAF

PEOPLE   ALL OVER   USE   LIGHT FLASH

Nowadays, deaf people are using video relay services rather than TTYs.

Fingerspell "T-T-Y."

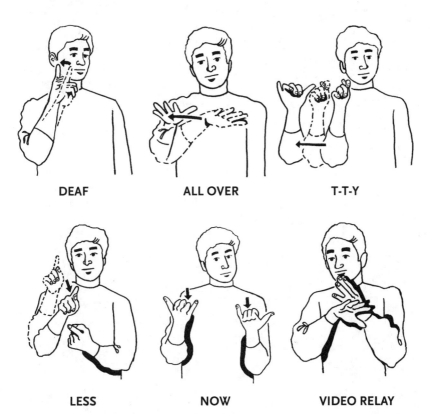

DEAF   ALL OVER   T-T-Y

LESS   NOW   VIDEO RELAY

APPENDIX

The Manual Alphabet

THE MANUAL ALPHABET allows us to fingerspell English words. When there is not a sign for an idea, then fingerspelling is used. This occurs most often with proper names. Mastery of fingerspelling is relatively easy if you form good habits from the very beginning.

First, relax your fingers. This may require bending and stretching the fingers so that they fall easily into the proper hand shapes. Next, relax your arm and shoulder. Tension is the greatest obstacle to clear formation of the letters, so strive to remain relaxed as you work at it. Let the arm hang down with the elbow to your side and the hand slightly in front of your body as the pictures show. Do not let your elbow start moving away from your side and rising upwards.

Rhythm is the most important quality to develop in fingerspelling. A rhythmical spelling is much easier to read than an unrythmical one, even when the letters are not perfectly formed. Rhythm is also critical for indicating when one word has ended and the next word has begun. This is done by holding on to the last letter of a word for about one-fourth of a beat of the rhythm you are using, then going on to the first letter of the next word. As you practice rhythmical fingerspelling, be sure you do not let the rhythm cause you to bounce your hand. Hold it steadily in one place.

Speed is not a goal to pursue. Work on rhythm, and then speed will come naturally in time. The tendency is to attempt to fingerspell too fast. Then the rhythm becomes broken when you cannot remember how to make a letter. A slow, rhythmic pattern is far more desirable than a fast but erratic rhythm.

Do not say the letters, either aloud or to yourself, as you make them. This is a very bad habit to get into and exceedingly hard to break once established. As you fingerspell a word, say the whole word. For instance, as you spell "C-A-T" do not say the letters, but say the word *cat*. You may say it aloud or without voice. It will seem awkward at first, but you will quickly become used to it.

The reason for speaking the word rather than saying the letters has to do with lipreading. Deaf people are taught to lipread words, not letters. When you fingerspell they see both your hand and your lips, and the two complement and reinforce each other. (This is also the reason you do not let your fingerspelling hand wander out to your side, too far away from your face.) It is not necessary to speak the word aloud; you may mouth it without using your voice.

When fingerspelling long words, pronounce the word syllable by syllable as you fingerspell it. For example, say, "fin" as you fin-gerspell "F-I-N," then say "ger" as you fingerspell "G-E-R," and then say "spell" as you fingerspell "S-P-E-L-L." (Double letters are moved slightly to the side or bumped back and forth slightly.) Caution: Do not pause after each syllable, but keep the rhythm flowing.

Practice spelling words, not just running through the alphabet. Begin with three-letter words, then work your way up to longer ones. A first-grade reading book provides excellent practice material because most of the words are short and are repeated often. Practice fingerspelling as you read a newspaper, listen to the radio or television, and see street signs and billboards. You may get some odd looks from some people, but never mind, you are on the road to mastering an intricate skill.

You will find that fingerspelling is much easier to do than to read. This happens because, initially, you tend to look for each individual letter as it is fingerspelled to you so that when you reach the end of the word you cannot make sense of the letters. You must learn to see whole words, not individual letters, just as you are doing as you read this printed material. You will have to find someone to learn and practice fingerspelling with you, since you cannot practice reading your own fingerspelling. As the two of you practice, do not speak or mouth the words since you would then hear or lipread them instead of reading the fingerspelling.

Here, in summary, are the tips to follow:

1. Relax.
2. Keep your elbow in and your hand in front of you.
3. Maintain a constant rhythm, but do not bounce your hand.
4. Pause for one-fourth of a beat at the end of each word.
5. Do not try to fingerspell rapidly.
6. Mouth or speak the word, not the letters.
7. Practice with someone so you can gain experience reading fingerspelling. (In this kind of practice, do not mouth or speak the word aloud.)
8. Look for the whole word, not individual letters.

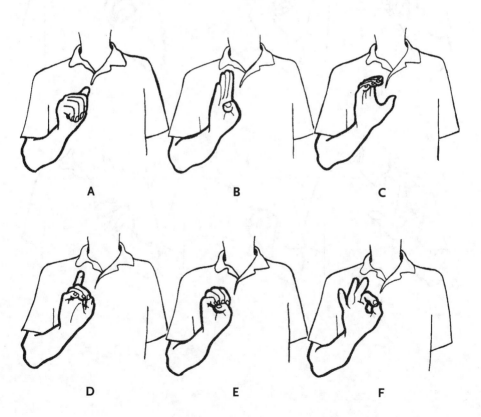

A   B   C

D   E   F

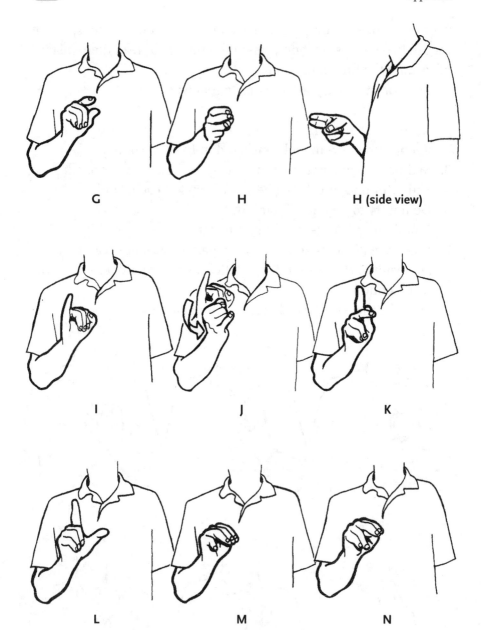

G

H

H (side view)

I

J

K

L

M

N

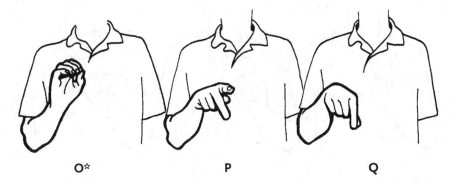

O*   P   Q

*Note: The sign for the letter *O* is the same as that for the number "0" (zero).

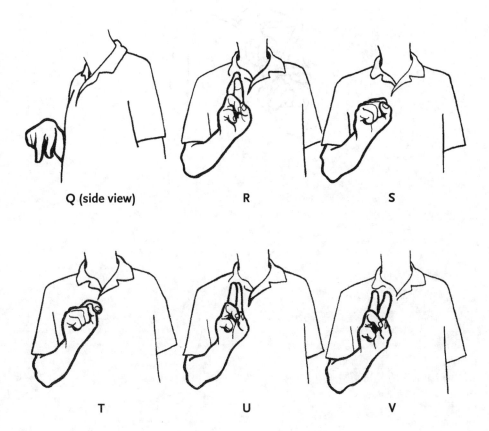

Q (side view)   R   S

T   U   V

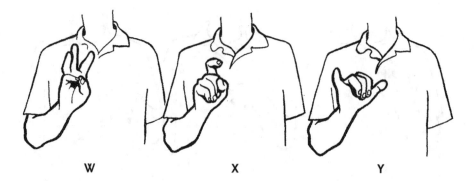

W   X   Y

Z

Dictionary/Index

THE DICTIONARY/INDEX consists of a combination of three things:

1. All the signs in this book listed by sign labels. All sign labels are in capital letters. When the meaning of the sign is not evident from the sign label, additional definitions and explanations are given.

2. English words that are glossed by signs in this book. The word is printed in lowercase letters, and the correct sign is in all capitals within parentheses following the word. Example: food (EAT). It is suggested that you refer to the sign label in the Dictionary/Index to see if an additional definition or explanation is given before looking up the picture of the sign.

3. Topics that are discussed in various sections of this book. They are printed as titles. Examples: "Past, Present, Future," "Labeling of the Drawings."

Abbreviations used:

SM: Single movement. The movement of the sign is made only once.
DM: Double movement. The movement of the sign is repeated once.